D0099061

WHITE JACKET REQUIRED

A CULINARY COMING-OF-AGE STORY

JENNA WEBER

AUTHOR OF THE BLOG *Eat, Live, Run*

STERLING EPICURE
New York

STERLING EPICURE
New York

An Imprint of Sterling Publishing
387 Park Avenue South
New York, NY 10016

STERLING EPICURE is a trademark of Sterling Publishing Co., Inc.
The distinctive Sterling logo is a registered trademark of Sterling Publishing Co., Inc.

© 2012 by Jenna Weber

All rights reserved. No part of this publication may be reproduced,
stored in a retrieval system, or transmitted, in any form or by any means,
electronic, mechanical, photocopying, recording, or otherwise,
without prior written permission from the publisher.

ISBN 978-1-4027-7777-6

Library of Congress Cataloging-in-Publication Data

Weber, Jenna.
  White jacket required : a culinary coming-of-age story / Jenna Weber.
    p. cm.
  ISBN 978-1-4027-7777-6 (hardback) -- ISBN 978-1-4027-9378-3 (ebook)
  1. Weber, Jenna. 2. Food writers--United States--Biography. 3. Cooking,
American. 4. Cordon Bleu Cookery School. I. Title.
  TX649.W435A3 2012
  641.5973092--dc23
  [B]
                    2012010845

Distributed in Canada by Sterling Publishing
$^{c}/o$ Canadian Manda Group, 165 Dufferin Street
Toronto, Ontario, Canada M6K 3H6
Distributed in the United Kingdom by GMC Distribution Services
Castle Place, 166 High Street, Lewes, East Sussex, England BN7 1XU
Distributed in Australia by Capricorn Link (Australia) Pty. Ltd.
P.O. Box 704, Windsor, NSW 2756, Australia

For information about custom editions, special sales, and premium and
corporate purchases, please contact Sterling Special Sales at 800-805-5489
or specialsales@sterlingpublishing.com.

Manufactured in the United States of America

2 4 6 8 10 9 7 5 3 1

www.sterlingpublishing.com

To my brother

I miss you more than
you could ever know.

CONTENTS

PROLOGUE

IN DECEMBER OF 2007, I STARTED A BLOG TO SHARE MY PASSION for food and my experiences as a new culinary student. In addition to the blog, I began keeping a detailed journal of interesting conversations with chef-instructors and fellow students, dreaming that someday these might become part of an actual book.

For as long as I can remember, all I really wanted to do in life was write about food, and I figured culinary school was the best place to start. After much debate, I decided to name my blog "Eat, Live, Run" to depict a healthy balance of food, life, and play. In the beginning, I only had three readers: my mom, my dad, and my roommate. However, as time went by and I kept at it, I was shocked to discover that people loved reading my blog as much as I loved writing it. Soon, my three readers multiplied into three hundred, and then into the thousands. As the years went by, I transitioned from blogging about culinary school to blogging about life in general, until I finally found my passion and niche for writing tasty, family-friendly recipes.

When I was given the opportunity to write a book, I couldn't wait to dive in. As much as I loved writing the blog, I was so excited to show my readers a deeper side of my life and share my experiences from culinary school and the year that followed. This book aims to do just that.

INTRODUCTION

France, 2007

DESPITE IT BEING MID-JULY, THE AIR WAS CHILLY IN PARIS AS I made my way to a travel-writing workshop. The walk was a little over a mile and scenic, with pastry shops, *crêperies*, and crumbling buildings scattering the streets on the Left Bank. Usually I would just eat a cold bowl of muesli in my apartment before starting my walk, but I was out of milk and hadn't had time yet to stop at the store. Hunger knotted my stomach, and I decided to stop at my favorite bakery just past Rue Mouffetard, on the way to the Paris American Academy campus on Rue St. Jacques.

The shop, called Pain au Naturel, was known for its organic and natural breads. I loved the small hazelnut rolls most of all. They were only about the size of my fist, hard and crusty on the outside, with a chewy interior studded with raw hazelnuts. The nuts gave the rolls an almost lavender color. I liked mine best torn apart and dunked in a frothy cappuccino.

I shifted my backpack on my shoulder and got in line outside the bakery. It was only 8:30 a.m., but the shelves behind the register were quickly emptying as people grabbed their morning croissants and rolls. Although I had taken five years of French in school prior to coming to Paris, I was still very much a rookie in the language and only knew a few food-related phrases that I felt confident using.

I often found myself in large crowds, not having any real idea what was being said around me.

When at last I made it inside, I smelled yeast, fire, and toast. A short, heavyset woman behind the register was taking people's money and handing them loaves at an astounding pace. When it was finally my turn, I spoke in slow, broken French.

"*J'aimerais un rouleau aux noisettes, s'il vous plaît,*" I said, the syllables feeling thick and twisted on my tongue. I handed the woman my two euros in exchange for a roll and thanked her before hustling back through the line and out of the shop.

As I continued to walk toward school, nibbling on my roll, I couldn't help but wonder about the life the woman in the bakery led. The idea of it was so strange to me, coming from a family where everyone worked in PR and marketing. It was always assumed that after I finished college I would move home and get a job at an agency, perhaps as a copywriter. I dreamed of someday writing my own books, maybe even a cookbook, but had no idea how to get there.

An ad for Le Cordon Bleu hung in the entrance to the next Métro stop, depicting a smiling woman wearing a tall chef's hat. *How cool that would be,* I thought, *to go to Le Cordon Bleu just like Julia Child did.* I could only imagine what life for the students would be like as they baked bread and learned classical French cooking techniques day in and day out. Of course I could never go. I hadn't heard much about culinary school, except that it was ridiculously expensive. Plus, I was just about to graduate from college. It would be silly to jump back into school now, without getting a bit of job experience first.

I thought back to the time two years before when I had practically begged my parents to let me drop out of college and go to culinary school instead. I had sunk into some late-teenage funk, and had grown bored of lecture halls and fraternity row. I had called my parents from a school psychologist's office in tears, telling them I wasn't cut out for this and that my heart told me culinary school was a much better option. They talked me out of it, and I was glad they did. Instead of dropping out of college altogether, I ended up taking a leave of absence before transferring to a different school. I found happiness at the College of Charleston, on the shores of South Carolina, and absolutely loved my time there.

The idea of culinary school still intrigued me, though. It was like an itch I couldn't scratch, especially here, where I was surrounded by beautiful Parisian bakeries and *pâtisseries*. I envied the bakers, who would probably never have to work in a drab cubicle or write copy for real estate agencies. As I ate the last crumbs of my hazelnut roll, in a foreign city an ocean away from home, I wondered if there was some way I could make the baker's life my own.

1
ORIGINS

WHEN I WAS GROWING UP, THE KITCHEN WAS A PLACE of comfort to me. My mom tells me that when I was little, my favorite seat in the house was a large wicker basket that I would place on the kitchen floor and sit in as she prepared dinner. She would toss me strips of bell pepper and chunks of baked potato, and I would happily sit and munch away. When I was five years old, my parents took me out to my first fancy meal at the Williamsburg Inn, in Williamsburg, Virginia, where we lived. I was given a high chair and a children's menu but vehemently beat my spoon against the table until I was given what I really wanted: the wild mushroom soup. From that moment on, I was officially classified as a foodie by the grown-ups around me. I was a child who was always eager to try anything on my parents' plates. When normal children were eating peanut butter on white bread, I was nibbling on risotto and Brie. I ate frozen peas straight from the bag as if they were candy.

When I officially outgrew the basket, I started to create my first culinary masterpieces straight out of *Little House on the Prairie*. I threw my eight-year-old efforts into producing hardtack (a flat, hard cracker eaten by soldiers during the Civil War), white bread (I was still unsure of the role of yeast), and rock-hard biscuits. My favorite thing to do in the kitchen was experiment, and it was not uncommon for me to add drops of green food coloring to my baked goods or create new forms of edible playdough or homemade glue (simply flour and water). My mom acted in the role of *sous-chef* and followed me around with a sponge and water, scrubbing at dried spots of pea-green dough and dustings of flour.

My dad, on the other hand, never really took part in the culinary activities. He was from a small town in Texas and a house of all boys. His mother—my grandmother—despised cooking and often would give each boy a plate and tell them to ring the neighbor's doorbell to get dinner *du jour*. Because of his lack of culinary upbringing, later in life he made it a point to find a wife who could cook. After a series of horrendous dates, he became a flight attendant for TWA in an effort to travel the world and (he hoped) meet a quality woman. Luckily, he met my mother. They were set up by mutual friends while living in a coastal suburb of Los Angeles. My mother was a flight attendant as well, and in an effort to impress her, my dad made quiche in a blender on their first date. He lived in a shoebox-size apartment in Los Angeles, and it was the only recipe he knew. My mom, having come from a tight-knit Midwestern family and a long line of great cooks, simply smiled, nodded, and ate the quiche, which couldn't have been *that* bad, since they've been married now for about thirty years.

Throughout my whole childhood, my mom cooked. She had grown up in Milwaukee, and her grandparents on both sides were immigrants. They passed down recipes and lore from Norway, Poland, and Germany, which my mother ultimately passed down to me. Scandinavian treats were the norm in my house during the Christmas holidays, and my favorite of these treats were the light, airy cookies called *rosettes*. Every December we baked rosettes in the shapes of stars and snowflakes on the traditional rosette iron that my grandmother had passed down to us. When the cookies had puffed up into a golden caramel color, we quickly peeled them off the iron and dusted them with powdered sugar. I had a bad habit of burning the tips of my fingers on the hot iron in an effort to pull the cookies off without breaking them, but the end result was always worth it. In addition to the rosettes, my mother always made homemade *crêpes* with strawberry sauce on Christmas morning while my brother and I opened all the gifts under the tree. The *crêpes* were so thin you could almost see right through them, and I loved mine with extra strawberries and a big dollop of fresh whipped cream. There were also miniature Swedish meatballs and gingerbread cookies made from a recipe perfected in my great grandmother's Minnesota kitchen.

When I was nine years old, my mom decided my passion for cooking was completely out of her hands and enrolled me in a summer cooking class for kids, along with my best friend, Helen; her twin brother, John; and our friend Ashleigh. It was that summer that my passion for cooking really began.

The class was taught by a tall, older Asian woman with short black hair and wire-rimmed glasses. She spoke with a thick Chinese accent and, ironically, didn't really seem to like children very much. She had little patience and was very serious about disciplined cooking. I didn't mind, though, because I was just so happy to finally be free to make food on my own, without my mom peering over my shoulder. Three afternoons each week, we met at the local public school in an empty classroom that was set up with Bunsen burners and a few pots and pans. Large tables filled the room, and construction-paper pies and cakes decorated the walls. I shared a table with my three friends. Miss Kim was constantly telling us to stop chatting, and when she wasn't looking we would make funny faces behind her back.

During that monthlong class, we made a wide variety of foods, from Belgian waffles to fried rice. We made jumbo chocolate chip cookies (and ate scoops of the creamy, chocolate-studded batter when Miss Kim wasn't watching); omelets with cheddar cheese; Hawaiian salad full of marshmallows and pineapple bits; and a delicious cereal concoction called "Puppy Chow," made with rice cereal, chocolate, peanut butter, and powdered sugar. We all took turns at the micro-wave, carefully melting our chocolate chips in glass-bottomed bowls. My favorite part, though, was slowly pouring the chocolate over the cereal in a long, thin stream. Of course, I also loved rolling up my sleeves and mixing everything by hand, chocolate getting underneath my fingernails and into the lines on my palms.

After class, Helen and I would race back to my house and remake what we'd made earlier, eagerly perfecting the art of cracking an egg into steaming grains of fried rice or creaming butter and sugar together to make chocolate-chip cookie dough. My favorite thing to make in class was delicate, crisp *pizzelle* cookies. They were made on an iron, just like the rosettes that I knew from home, but the Italian *pizzelle* also had a slight taste of licorice.

For my friends and me, cooking began to become something of a social activity. Instead of going over to someone's house to play, we would go over to someone's house to cook. Helen, Ashleigh, and I would often dress up like Laura Ingalls Wilder or Kirsten, the pioneer girl from the American Girls series. Sometimes we pretended we were on a ship sailing to America from Europe; we were cooks working in the ship's galley. I begged my grandmother to sew me pioneer and pilgrim apparel to wear just for fun, and I took much joy in fastening my tiny petticoat (with ruffles on the end!), lacing up my boots, and tying my apron tight.

If my parents ever questioned their young daughter's mental wellness, they never said anything, just smiled and let me do my thing. On a few occasions, I would go as far as taking all the dirty laundry (or what I *thought* was dirty laundry) to the woods behind my house and then proceed to wash the clothes by hand, with homemade soap that I concocted using an old-time recipe. A few times I cut up green apples into very thin slices, threaded them onto string, and hung them all around the laundry room, to dry for winter. This being the 1990s, there was absolutely no need for me to ration food for winter, but I wanted so badly to be Laura Ingalls Wilder that I took matters into my own hands.

Of course, fantasizing about living in a different century was a childhood phase, but parts of it never really left me. Even as a teenager living in Florida, I would find myself rereading the *Little House on the Prairie* books in secret and being undeniably drawn to all aspects of frontier life. I loved to wear my long blond hair in two braids and took to old-fashioned activities such as horseback riding, knitting, and baking. I always insisted on baking my own birthday cake every year, and chose elaborate Victorian-style cakes with boiled frosting or meringue—the more layers to the cake, the better. I bought my first candy thermometer when I was fourteen and spent hours by the stove, perfecting the soft ball stage of boiling sugar and water together to create homemade ribbon candy.

Every night growing up, my family ate a homemade dinner together at 6:30 with candles on the table and, oftentimes, in the morning, a homemade breakfast as well. Mom loved to try new recipes, and dinners were healthy by most standards. We lived in a small resort town right on the Atlantic, and I grew up packing my little brother into our big red wagon, along with a bag of puffed rice and the family beagle, and setting out on elaborate "adventures" around the golf course that we lived on. After about two hours of forging new trails along the prairie, we got back just in time for dinner, which was usually chicken, seafood, or pasta. Seafood was easy since we lived in a place where fresh fish were caught daily. Because of this, we never ate too much beef—maybe a steak once a month, if that.

My absolute favorite dish was always linguine with clams. My mom used canned clams from the store and finished the dish with a squeeze of lemon, a sprinkle of Parmesan cheese, and hot chili flakes for heat. I would always push all my clams to the side of my plate and save them for last. I loved the salty, briny taste and the way they squeaked between my teeth. Still to this day, linguine and clams is my number-one favorite meal to request when I go home, and though I've tried countless times to re-create my mom's version, I can never hit it just right on my own.

When I finally moved out of my parents' house for college, I craved the familiarity of mealtime and the feeling of fitting in with a group. Going from nightly meals straight out of *Gourmet* and *Bon Appétit* to frozen Lean Cuisine and cereal was a rude awakening. I despised the dining hall on campus, and some days I was so homesick that it felt like my heart was breaking. None of the other students in there seemed to really care what they were eating and filled up on mashed potatoes from a box, greasy burgers, and fries. No one talked about food except to say that you should always eat dinner before going to the bars so that the food would soak up the alcohol. I never drank in high school, and the first time I did, I ended up vomiting all over the bathroom floor. I couldn't understand the big fuss over getting drunk, and that only seemed to further separate me from my fellow freshmen. The only place I really felt like I fit in was the library, so while all the other girls in my hall took turns taking shots before going to campus parties, I would hide behind my books and question whether I was really born in the right century.

My mom would send me care packages full of pieces of home— black-licorice dogs, cinnamon gummy bears, and faded recipes on old note cards. Of course, I had to wait to actually cook the recipes that she sent, but sometimes just running my fingers along the worn edges of the paper seemed to help in a tiny way. After feeling out of place for a year, I transferred to the College of Charleston—someplace much closer to my Florida home.

We'd lived in the Lowcountry for a while when I was very young, and in moving to Charleston as an adult I came to find what seemed to be a missing piece of my own puzzle. The town itself was old and historic, with cobblestoned roads and horse-drawn carriages. I could hear the clopping of the horses' hooves outside my window in the early evenings, and it gave me a sense of peace. Since I was an English major with a concentration in creative writing, my department was small and my classes consisted of about ten students sitting in a circle workshopping pieces of their writing. Gone were the days of lecture and dining halls filled with hundreds of students. Restaurants and cafés lined King Street all the way down to the South Battery, and I made new friends who loved food as much as I did. Instead of going to sorority parties, we would gather at quaint coffee shops and restaurants and talk about food for hours, then go back to our apartments and cook meals for each other.

Every Saturday in Miriam Square Park, there was a huge farmers' market filled with colorful booths of fruits and vegetables. Local vendors sold handmade soaps, jewelry, and other wares. I loved to walk down to the market early and buy a sweet Nutella *crêpe* to eat while I walked around. The hazelnut chocolate was spread so thick that it stuck to the inside of my teeth and occasionally got in my hair as I walked. The scent of coffee and fried dough hung in the air as locals filled their cloth bags with ripe eggplants, peppers, and cherries. For the first time in my life, I was able to taste the difference between produce from the grocery store and produce straight from the farm. At the time, eating local and organic was a relatively new concept that had hit Charleston with full force, and I embraced it wholeheartedly. I bought lettuce that had just been pulled up from the ground that morning, and I also bought fresh Carolina shrimp and local honey.

Foodies and chefs seemed to be more focused on using the freshest ingredients possible than anything nonfat and low-calorie, and that was more than fine with me. Unlike some of the college girls I knew, I never really fell prey to fad diets or eating disorders. When my old college sorority sisters were keeping up with the latest diet craze—100-calorie packs of Oreos, for example—I was snacking on a handful of raw almonds instead. I found that I was able to stay slim by eating small portions of whatever I chose, and I always sought out food made with the highest-quality ingredients. Charleston was right up my alley.

Linguine and Clam Sauce

Serves 4

Hands down, my favorite dish. Since there's no need to buy fancy live clams from the seafood counter, you can make this year-round.

8 ounces dried linguine
1 tablespoon extra-virgin olive oil
1 large shallot, minced
3 (6.5 ounce) cans clams, drained, with ½ cup juice reserved
Juice of one lemon
¼ teaspoon red pepper flakes (or to taste)
½ cup freshly grated Parmesan cheese

Cook the pasta in boiling salted water until *al dente*. Drain and set aside.

Heat olive oil in a large pan over medium-high heat until it shimmers. Add minced shallot and sauté until very soft and tender, about 5 minutes.

Add clams and continue to cook for another 3 to 4 minutes. Add reserved clam juice, lemon juice, and red pepper flakes. Bring to a simmer and cook for 3 minutes.

Toss pasta with sauce, adjusting red pepper flakes to taste. Divide among four plates and serve with freshly grated Parmesan cheese on top.

All-Occasion Yellow Cake

Serves 8

A simple yet delicious cake that comes together in less than 45 minutes. If you prefer, you can make fluffy cupcakes instead (standard-size cupcakes will take about 30 minutes to bake). And, don't forget the chocolate frosting!

1 cup all-purpose flour
1½ teaspoons baking powder
½ teaspoon salt
½ stick (4 tablespoons) butter, softened
½ cup plus 2 tablespoons sugar
1 egg
2 teaspoons vanilla extract
⅓ cup milk
Chocolate-Buttercream Frosting (recipe follows)
Rainbow sprinkles

Preheat oven to 350°F and grease a 9-inch cake pan.

In a medium-size bowl, combine the flour, baking powder, and salt. Set aside.

Cream together the butter and sugar. Add the egg and beat until combined. Add the vanilla extract and beat again.

Add the dry ingredients alternately with the milk to the butter/sugar mixture and mix until smooth.

Scoop batter into the greased cake pan and bake until light, springy, and golden, about 25 minutes. Transfer to a cake rack to cool for 5 minutes, then invert cake onto a rack to cool completely.

Frost the cake with chocolate buttercream and top with rainbow sprinkles.

Chocolate-Buttercream Frosting

1 stick (8 tablespoons) unsalted butter, at room temperature
3 cups powdered sugar
Pinch of sea salt
2 teaspoons vanilla
3 tablespoons cocoa powder
2 tablespoons milk

In the bowl of an electric mixer, cream together the butter, powdered sugar, salt, and vanilla for 5 minutes on high speed. Add the cocoa powder and milk and keep beating for another 8–10 minutes until very light, thick, and fluffy.

2
MAKE IT HAPPEN

WHEN I FINISHED COLLEGE AND MY SUMMER IN PARIS came to an end, I moved in with my parents in Tampa to figure out what to do next. It felt odd to be completely away from papers and exams once and for all, and I found myself missing school more than anticipated. I was at loose ends without the structure that college had provided. Although I was happy to finally be living in the same city as Rob, my boyfriend of two years, I somehow felt more alone than I had in a long time.

Rob and I had met in an elevator (of all places) the summer before my senior year of college and had maintained a long-distance relationship ever since. He was eight years older than I was, and although we were polar opposites in just about every way, we always managed to have a great time together. Moving back home not only meant living three miles from him, but also sharing a bathroom once again with my teenage brother, John, my only sibling. John and I had our fair share of differences (often resulting in screaming battles), but I was excited to be there for him as he made his way through high school.

At my parents' house, I spent my days on Monster.com looking for jobs. The initial excitement of the hunt gave way to frustration, and after scouring job listings for weeks to no avail (except for one interview for a writing position offering to pay me $6 an hour), I felt ready to give up. I was working part-time again at Anthropologie, a popular women's clothing and home store where I had worked for a month before heading to Paris, so at least I was bringing in a little income. But I failed to be mentally stimulated after folding clothes all day.

One August evening, I sought the wisdom and advice of my mother. I was helping her chop vegetables for her famous spaghetti sauce, a dish I almost always requested whenever I was at home.

I was quiet and distant as I diced the carrots and celery, easing them off the edge of the granite counter and into a metal bowl.

My mom glanced over at me. "Jenny, what is it that you really love to do?" she asked.

I ate a carrot. "Well, obviously write . . . and eat. I just don't know how to combine those two and actually make a career out of them."

My mom smiled. "Do you know how lucky you are, though? While so many college graduates have no idea what it is they really want to do, you know exactly! Now all you have to do is make it happen!"

Make it happen. As if anything was that easy. It turns out no one wants to hire a recent graduate with zero experience. I knew how lucky I was to have my parents be able to support me while I hunted for a job, but I also knew that their compassion would only extend so far.

"What if . . . I went to culinary school?" I asked, turning my face back toward the vegetables, not believing it was my voice that actually posed the question out loud. Since discussing it with my parents a few years prior, I hadn't brought it up, and I wasn't really sure how they would react. I also still didn't know much about culinary school, other than that Julia Child did it, and that it was expensive. It had always seemed more reasonable to go to graduate school and get my master's degree, but I'd had a horrible experience with the GRE that past spring and had thrown out my practice book in protest.

"What if? Is that what you really want to do?" my mom asked as she continued to stir the sauce on the stove.

"I know that I want more education and that I love to cook. If I went, it would give me the authority to *really* write about food because then I would really know my subject." I was excited now at the thought. Visions of cupcakes and croissants floated through my head, as did cute white aprons and amazing dinners.

"Well, look into it then. You know though that your dad and I can't support any further education that you take on. If you want to do this, you need to figure out all the details, and I'm sure it's pretty expensive."

As the spaghetti sauce simmered in the pot, so did the ideas in my head. I knew there was a Cordon Bleu school about an hour away, in Orlando, but I didn't know a thing about it. If I went, where would I live? What would I do for work? I decided to sleep on it and do some Internet research in the morning. Lots of people went to culinary school, and I always did like a challenge.

My Mother's Spaghetti Sauce

serves 6–8

Rumor has it that my mother came by this spaghetti sauce recipe from a certain old boyfriend, but my dad won't speak of that. Anyway, it's a family favorite. Try to make it a day or so ahead of time to allow the flavors to blend. Should there be any leftovers, the sauce freezes beautifully.

> **Chopped vegetables: mushrooms, onions, green pepper, red
>   pepper**
> **1½ tablespoons olive oil**
> **1½ pounds ground beef**
> **3 hot Italian sausages, chopped**
> **1 (28-ounce) can tomato purée**
> **1 (12-ounce) can tomato paste**
> **3 (8-ounce) cans tomato sauce (two with herbs, one regular)**
> **6 ounces freshly grated Romano Cheese**
> **½ cup red wine**
> **Dash each: oregano, basil, salt, pepper, garlic salt, sugar, bay leaf**

Sauté vegetables in the olive oil in a large skillet over medium heat. Add the beef and sausages and cook until browned. Add the tomato purée, tomato paste, tomato sauce, cheese, red wine, and spices and simmer for an hour and a half, uncovered, stirring occasionally.

3
FACT FINDING

E CORDON BLEU COLLEGE OF CULINARY ARTS IN ORLANDO, Florida, is located right off a major highway, behind a fast-food burger joint. The building is large but unassuming; its only identifying feature is the royal-blue sign above the entrance. As I pulled up for my first visit, students dressed all in white milled around the parking lot, smoking cigarettes, drinking coffee, and eating hot dogs from the school cafeteria. Upon first glance, it surely wasn't the eighteenth-century French mansion that I had imagined; there were no chimneys or lovely windowpanes. The dull roar of interstate traffic could still be heard as I approached the building.

When I got inside, I was again a little disappointed. In my romantic vision of culinary school, I had pictured chefs whirling in and out of shiny industrial kitchens, carrying fresh-baked croissants, possibly on silver platters. Instead, I saw the Food Network playing on flat-screen TVs and women dressed in business suits answering phone calls and directing people to the waiting area for the school tour. No croissants or silver platters, and the air smelled faintly of old paint. I had signed up to go on the tour alone because my parents were out of the country on vacation and Rob was working, and I was anxious to see what the school was really like. So far, I wasn't that impressed. I glanced at my watch. The tour would start in five minutes. Then, I would meet an old friend for a late bite to eat down the street, before heading back to Tampa.

Five other people were waiting in the office with me. Three of them looked to be about eighteen and reminded me of my brother. They wore baggy jeans and wrinkled polo shirts and seemed to know the girl who worked behind the desk. Around their necks hung blue lanyards and photo IDs with the traditional Le Cordon Bleu logo. The girl they were flirting with was blushing. She whispered something in Spanish and shooed them away with her hand. The boys laughed and disappeared through the double doors. That left me alone with a woman and a boy.

The admissions girl stood up. "Anyone going on the one o'clock tour, please follow me! I'm Cherie and I'll be your tour guide today," she said. "What are your names, please?"

"I'm Jenna," I said.

"I'm Laurie," said the woman next to me.

The guy barely mumbled, "Casey."

"Nice to meet you all," Cherie said. "The tour will take about forty-five minutes, and then afterward, if you want to stick around, I can answer any questions you might have. We'll go into a few kitchens, meet some chefs, and help you get to know Le Cordon Bleu!" Cherie smiled and then pushed open the double doors with her back, revealing a whole new world. Students with black-and-white checkered pants and starched white coats moved quickly down the halls and into classrooms on the right and left. Aromas of meat and garlic filled the air, and chefs with tall hats walked with authority. I tried to picture myself here, wearing those baggy pants and the highly unflattering white cap. I was skeptical. As Cherie stopped to chat with a chef for a moment, Laurie moved to my side. "So, what's your story?" she asked as we peered into a classroom kitchen and saw students with notebooks in their hands huddling around a chef-instructor. The students were scribbling furiously while the chef held a whole raw chicken in the air.

"Well, I just graduated from College of Charleston up in South Carolina. I have an English degree, but what I've always wanted to do is write about food, so I thought culinary school would give me a good background for that."

"A food writer? Neat! I always though those restaurant critics up there in New York City had the best jobs. I mean, to eat for free!" Laurie said excitedly. She spoke with a bit of a Southern accent, and I guessed she was from closer to the Alabama state line, up in the Panhandle.

I laughed and nodded. "Yeah well, I don't really want to be a critic, although free meals would be nice. I always wanted to write books on food, actually, like cookbooks or novels with recipes in them."

"Well, good luck! I've never heard of anyone going to culinary school to be a writer, but it sounds interesting all right," Laurie said and then added with a whisper, "This place sure is expensive, I'll tell you!"

Expensive, indeed. The tuition for both the Culinary and the Baking and Pastry programs rang in around $40,000. I hadn't told my parents too much about the school yet, but knew that if I wanted to go, it would be out of my own pocket by means of student loans.

Laurie told me that it was her lifelong dream to own a bakery, and she was finally in a position to make it come true now that all her children had grown up and moved out. Her passion was cake decorating, and she was interested in the Baking and Pastry program. Laurie had gotten pregnant right out of high school and had been a stay-at-home mom for the past twenty-two years.

Casey, on the other hand, didn't speak at all throughout the entire tour other than to mumble the occasional *yeah* or *I dunno*. He had a tribal tattoo around his forearm and wore his jeans three inches lower on his waist than advised.

All of a sudden, Cherie turned around and paused. "We're going to walk into this classroom kitchen now, so that you all can get a glimpse of what really goes on behind the scenes here. This is Chef Jason's Basic Skills Two class, and I think the students are about to eat dessert—you all are in luck!"

Inside, the air smelled of vanilla and burnt sugar; about ten students stood around a long metal table. There were slices of what appeared to be cheesecake on small white plates and squeeze bottles full of bright red liquid (raspberry sauce?) scattered around. Dishes were stacked up near the sink in the back, and the tables were filled with knives, spoons, and metal whisks. The students were chatting amongst themselves while the chef sat in the back, typing on a desktop computer. For the first time that afternoon, things started to seem real to me, and I was excited to be in on the action. Our tour guide asked one of the students if he could explain to us what they were making.

"Well, we just finished making Beef Wellington, and now this here is New York–style cheesecake with raspberry coulis." He gestured toward the slice of cake on the plate in front him, clearly very proud of his creation. "Y'all want to try a bite? It's real good, I promise!" He handed out forks to the three of us and smiled. Never being one to turn down dessert, I immediately dug my fork in. The cheesecake was thick and rich, with a lovely tang.

"This is fantastic!" I said enthusiastically as I took a bite of the graham cracker crust. It really *was* fantastic, and at that moment I felt for the first time that this could really be the right place for me. Baking cheesecake all day? I could certainly handle that.

The tour ended with us back at the admissions office, and I said good-bye and good luck to Laurie as she headed out. "Think you'll be back?" she asked me.

I just shrugged. "We'll see! You never know!"

I pulled out of the school parking lot and drove to meet Helen, my childhood best friend. She had called me out of the blue a week ago and asked me if we could meet for lunch. We hadn't seen each other at all for about three years, and I was really looking forward to catching up. We'd met on a second-grade class trip to a science museum, and from that moment on, we were inseparable. When we were younger, our moms were best friends as well, and over the years we took count-less family vacations together. Most of my best childhood memories involved Helen. At one time, we had been as close as sisters, but after graduating from high school and heading away to college, we'd stopped being in constant communication. Our daily phone calls slowly turned into weekly, then monthly, and soon, we would chat only every few months, laughing about stories from when we were little, but lacking more recent shared experiences to talk about. I missed my best friend, but it just seemed as if we'd had more in common as preteens than we did now, as women entering adulthood. Still, I couldn't wait to see her and hear the latest news in her life. About two months earlier, my mom had told me that she talked to Helen's mother and learned that Helen was moving to Orlando to become a police officer. At the time, I laughed hysterically, not being able to picture sweet, beautiful Helen carrying a gun and a badge. I was anxious to get the full scoop today.

Helen jumped up from her seat and gave me a huge hug the moment I walked through the doors at P.F. Chang's.

"Hi!" I said with a big smile. "You look so gorgeous! I've missed you so much!"

Helen did look gorgeous, with her designer T-shirt, fashionable ripped jeans, and large Prada purse. "I want to hear everything!" she told me as we sat down.

"Well," I told her. "I'm in Orlando looking at going to culinary school, actually!"

Helen's eyes got wide. "Oh my God! You would be perfect for that! The culinary school over on the parkway?"

"Yeah, there's a Le Cordon Bleu there. I never really thought I would actually go, and I'm still pretty unsure, but I just finished going on the school tour. I've had it up to here sitting at home and looking for entry-level writing jobs online, you know?"

The waitress came by and set down a glass of water and lemon in front of me. I scanned the menu and quickly ordered some orange-peel shrimp, my favorite. Helen ordered a spicy noodle dish and a soda.

I took a long sip of water and picked up my fork. "But what about you?" I asked her. "I heard some rumor you are moving here to become . . . a cop?!" I raised my eyebrows incredulously.

Helen giggled. "I am! Can you even believe it? Well, I graduated from the police academy last month and got placed here right after. I'm supposed to start my job in two months and I'm looking at apartments like crazy right now."

I still couldn't get it through my head that Helen, little Helen from down the street, was going to be a police officer. Something about it just didn't add up in my mind. "I had no idea you were serious when you said you wanted to work with the police! What does your mother think about all this?"

Helen sighed and made a face. "You know Mom. All she does is worry. I mean, of course she wishes I had chosen a safer career, but I really want to help people and this seems like the best way."

Our meals came, and the serious talk ended as we dug into our lunch. My shrimp were perfect, slightly spicy and crusted with chewy orange peel. I cleaned my plate in about five minutes flat.

"You know," Helen said, "if you were actually serious about this culinary school thing and were planning on moving here, we could totally live together."

I looked up from my plate. "I didn't even think of that," I said.

When we were kids, Helen and I made a pact that we would be roommates when we were finally old enough to get our own place. I hadn't thought about that for at least fifteen years.

"Remember how we always said we would be roommates some-day?" she asked, excitement growing in her voice. "We always said we would live where it snowed and have a little house."

I laughed. "I was actually just thinking the exact same thing. We also said we would have a big furry dog! It sure isn't about to snow any time soon here in Orlando, but yes, I remember."

The rest of lunch was spent gossiping about friends we went to middle school with and discussing potential future apartments. I still hadn't made up my mind, but now that I knew Helen was going to be there and wanted to live together, the idea of moving seemed much more feasible. When we said good-bye, I promised to call her immediately after I talked to my family and made a decision. She was heading to look at one more apartment that afternoon before driving home to Naples, and she promised to keep me updated as well.

During the next few weeks, I thought long and hard about going back to school. I weighed the pros and cons and discussed the matter at length with Rob. He urged me to go, saying it was a once-in-a-lifetime opportunity and that we would work out the distance between us. My parents were supportive, but of course they reminded me that the tuition would come out of my own pocket. Finally, I decided to just go for it. It was only fifteen months, after all, and how could I turn down living in a new city with my best friend? I called Helen as I was faxing my paperwork over to the school, and we both starting screaming into the phone. She had found a nice two-bedroom apartment about four miles away from school, right next to the newest and nicest mall in Orlando. We set a move-in date three weeks away, and I started to pack.

A week later, I was back at Le Cordon Bleu, this time with my dad, to sign the final papers that would secure my place in the class of 2008.

"I know it's not much to look at from the outside," I told him as we walked toward the admissions office. "But it's like a whole different world inside, I promise!" We headed in, and once again the

Food Network was on, and women in business suits and telephone headsets answered calls behind the front desk. It felt different this time, though. This was my school now.

We signed in at the front desk, and after a short wait we were led back into the admissions office. An African American woman named Rhonda had been assigned to be my admissions coordinator and take care of things like uniforms, textbooks, and class schedules, as well as to help me finalize my new Sallie Mae loan. I had a feeling I wasn't really going to like Sallie Mae very much, but I chose to think about the present moment instead of the future.

"Jennifer! Welcome!" Rhonda's voice boomed, filling the small cubicle where my dad and I sat. When I asked her if she had completed the Culinary program herself, she just laughed and said that her husband did all the cooking in their house.

"I've got your three sets of uniforms all folded up for you right here, Jennifer. Why don't you go in the bathroom over there and try them on so we'll know if we need to make any changes." She signaled over to the left corner of the room where there was a water cooler and a tiny door. She set a pair of size small black-and-white checkered pants and a white chef coat in my arms, and the sheer weight of the outfit shocked me. Once in the bathroom, I struggled with the coat, pulling it in every direction, trying to get it to lie more flatteringly against my body. After a few minutes, I gave up and walked out self-consciously.

Rhonda and my dad were waiting right outside the door. "Now there's a real chef! You look great, girlfriend!" Rhonda exclaimed, pulling a bit on my coat. "Are you sure you don't want to get a size up, though? Most students do find that they gain about ten or fifteen pounds during the first few months of school. All that butter they use!"

My expression must have told it all, because my dad started laughing and he winked at me. "Oh no . . . " I laughed. "I don't really think I have to worry about that; I'm a pretty avid exerciser."

Rhonda shrugged. "You sure?" she asked.

"Oh yeah, I'm fine. These fit perfectly." I walked back into the bathroom and looked at my reflection in the small mirror. I felt like a whole different person. Gone were the days of cute sundresses and designer jeans. I was entering a whole new reality, one where I didn't have to worry every day about what to wear or how to do my hair. The thought was actually rather freeing.

The textbooks, standard-issue Le Cordon Bleu books that were given to students at every one of their fifty-some schools around the country, were large and heavy. Being a longtime reader and lover of cookbooks, I eagerly opened up *Cooking Fundamentals* on the ride home that afternoon and paged through some of the recipes. All of the ingredients were listed by weight instead of the standard cup and tablespoon measurements that I was used to, and I hoped that when I went to pick up my tool kit the week before classes started, a scale would be included. Unlike typical cookbooks, this one was geared toward a professional, or restaurant, kitchen. No pretty pictures and no novella-like paragraphs introducing the recipes, just simple ingredient lists and cooking methods. This cookbook was boring, and I was a little disappointed.

"Well, honey, I'm really excited for you," my dad said during the car ride home. "It seems as if this is where you're meant to be, and I'm proud of you for making the decision. I'm sure you know it's not all going to be easy, but I really think you're going to do great!"

"Thanks, Dad. I'm excited, too. Helen and I were talking last night about decorating the kitchen in the new place, and I just can't wait to move in." I think I was almost as excited to get my own apartment as I was to start school.

"Have you thought about a job yet?" Dad looked over at me. "You know your mother and I can help you out a little bit, but you still need to pull your own weight. We can pay for half of your rent, as we discussed, but everything else needs to come out of your own pocket. This is part of being an adult."

I let out a sigh. "I know, Dad! And you know I hate to ask for money, anyway. Finding a job will be the first thing I do, promise."

Once we got home, I packed my new textbooks and uniforms in a box, labeled it "Cordon Bleu" in big black letters, and shoved it in the hallway. I couldn't wait to start my new life.

Move-in day came just a week later and was filled with boxes, sweat, and hugs. Helen had hired professional movers to carry up all her old furniture from college, while I just plopped down two suitcases and three sealed boxes on the living room floor. I figured I wouldn't need too much, since I'd be wearing a chef uniform every day, so I left most of my belongings at home at my parents' house. Helen had generously offered me her old guest-room furniture, and I loved my new room with a view of downtown Orlando. That evening, after all the movers had gone and Helen and I were finally alone, we decided to go grab Pad Thai from a restaurant down the street. As we squeezed lime on our noodles and swirled them around our forks, we caught up on what had been happening in each other's lives during the past few years in college. I told her about transferring from University of Alabama to College of Charleston, dancing barefoot to beach music on the Carolina coast, and meeting Rob in an elevator the summer before. She told me about her crazy Tallahassee parties, the rigidness of the police academy, and how if she wasn't going to be a cop, she would have tried to become a fashion designer. By the end of the meal we were laughing so hard we were crying. Finally, our little-girl dream was coming true.

We spent the next few days by the apartment pool, soaking up the last of the summer sun and our freedom before my classes began and Helen started her new job. I had exactly three weeks to find a job, but I just wanted a few days to relax and get to know Helen again. Like me, she enjoyed cooking, so we made the traditional Greek recipes that she grew up on and that we both loved, like *avgolemono* soup and light, buttery cookies covered in powdered sugar. Helen was quiet, like me, and came from a good family. Her twin brother had just graduated from Babson, a business school in Boston, and was hoping to break into the real estate market.

"So, do you think that you and Rob will end up together?" Helen asked as she reached for the bottle of sunscreen. There were no clouds in the sky, an absolutely perfect late-summer afternoon.

I paused and thought for a second before I answered. "I honestly don't know. Sometimes I think so, sometimes I don't. We've never really talked about it, and I don't want to be one of those girls who just settles down right after college with her first serious boyfriend, you know?"

Helen nodded. She was dating another police officer, who lived a few hours away as well. They were serious, but I couldn't see them staying together. Helen had no intention of settling down in her early twenties, and this seemed to make all the guys want her even more. "Yeah, that's how I feel about Michael," she said. "I know he wants something super serious but I'm only twenty-two. I have to make a career for myself before anything else happens."

I pondered the word *career*. I was about to go back to school for another year and a half before even really starting mine. Rob was eight years older than I was, and most of his friends were already married, some of them with kids. Rob was mature and steadfast, with a good job in the financial field and an apartment of his own. He was at a place in his life where a serious relationship made sense. There were definitely times I thought about whether we would settle down together, but that was nothing I really wanted to get into right now. Despite the fact that I was a college graduate and was living on my own, I still felt very much like a kid at times.

"I know what you mean," I said. "Rob and I have a lot of fun together, but I just don't know who I'll even be in the future. . . . I could be a completely different person." I rolled onto my back, trying to focus on my first day of school instead of where I would be in the next five years. I preferred to take one day at a time, and right now, that meant remembering to unpack my schoolbooks.

That night, after we had eaten a simple, quick dinner of turkey burgers and sweet potato fries, I sat on the living room floor organizing my books while the Food Network played in the background. I never really got into the competitive cooking shows, always preferring *Giada* or *Paula Deen*, but that night I found myself wondering if school would be like a real-life episode of *Top Chef.* I had always been the quiet, introverted one in class, never raising my hand unless I was 110 percent sure I knew the correct answer. How would I fare being under pressure all the time? Just the thought of it gave me butterflies in my stomach. I stared down at the book in my lap, a book for Meat Fabrication, a class I knew absolutely nothing about. My future was completely unwritten, and I loved it that way.

Girls' Night Turkey Burgers with Spicy Sweet Potato Fries

Serves 2

Old Bay seasoning is the secret ingredient in these easy and healthy turkey burgers. I like to serve mine with melted cheddar or pepperjack cheese on top. The spicy sweet potato fries (baked of course!) complete the meal.

1 large sweet potato, peeled and sliced into matchstick-thin slices
Sea salt
⅛ teaspoon cayenne pepper, or to taste
Cooking oil spray
½ pound lean ground turkey
1 egg, lightly beaten
½ teaspoon sea salt
1 teaspoon Old Bay seasoning
1 red bell pepper, chopped
2 slices cheddar or pepperjack cheese (optional but delicious)
2 hamburger buns, toasted (preferably whole wheat)
Ketchup or hot sauce

Preheat the oven to 400°F and grease a cookie sheet.

Arrange the sweet potato slices in one layer on the sheet and sprinkle with sea salt and cayenne. Spray fries with vegetable oil spray and bake for 30 minutes, turning each fry over midway through baking.

In a large bowl, combine the turkey, egg, salt, Old Bay seasoning, and bell pepper. Mix thoroughly either with your hands or with a spoon until everything comes together and is combined well. Form into two even patties.

Cook the burgers in a nonstick skillet over moderate heat until cooked through, about 7 minutes per side. Top each with a slice of cheese and cook two minutes longer, allowing the cheese to melt.

Remove from heat and serve on toasted buns, topped with desired accompaniments. Serve with hot sweet potato fries and plenty of ketchup and hot sauce.

4

WORKING GIRLS

THE NEXT DAY I DUG OUT MY FAVORITE CASUAL BLACK DRESS from my suitcase, put on some makeup, and declared to Helen that I wasn't coming back until I had a job. She just nodded, ate her cereal, and continued to watch Paula Deen make cornbread.

I didn't really have a set list of places that I wanted to go, but I figured Orlando was a huge resort town with tons of restaurants, and I had plenty of experience waiting tables from my teenage years. I also figured that the fact I was about to start culinary school could only help my case, although I had no desire to actually work in the kitchen. All I was looking for was a nice, safe hostess position—something with hours that would work with my school schedule and still allow me to go home from time to time to see Rob and my family.

I drove over to Sand Lake Road, an area in Orlando known for its many restaurants, cafés, and shops. Disney World is only three miles away, and the whole community pretty much survives on tourism alone. As I drove under the interstate overpass, I saw throngs of tourists waiting for buses into the theme park, sunburn lines crisscrossing their backs. I had never lived in a city of this size before, and Orlando sometimes scared me with its crowds and constant bumper-to-bumper traffic.

I pulled into the parking lot at what appeared to be a busy and popular outdoor shopping center and scanned the restaurants. There was a high-end steak place, a sushi restaurant, a Middle Eastern café, and a Hawaiian restaurant named Roy's. I recognized the name and walked in. The restaurant was empty except for the chefs working behind the line of the open-air kitchen. Aromas of ginger and grilled meat permeated the restaurant's main room, and suddenly, I found myself very hungry.

"Are you here for Tony?" a deep voice shouted from the back.

"I'm, ummm, here to apply for a job. Do you know where I can find the manager?" I asked.

A small, middle-aged man dressed in a white chef coat came out of the kitchen. "Yeah, Tony. He's the owner. He just went around the corner for a coffee, but he should be back any minute. I'm Andrew, the head chef here. Why don't you take a seat? He shouldn't be long." Andrew handed me a menu to look at and gestured to a booth.

"Perfect. Thank you. I'm Jenna, by the way," I said as I took the menu and sat down to wait. Not five minutes later, Tony burst through the door, talking loudly on his cell phone and holding a tray of coffees.

"I don't care what she says. This is MY RESTAURANT and I MAKE THE RULES." He slammed his phone shut and muttered profanity under his breath. Feeling anxious now, I cleared my throat and thought about how he reminded me of my Basic Skills 1 chef-instructor, with whom I had spent three long hours earlier that day.

"Who are you?" Tony demanded. "Please tell me you're not here to sell me more wine; I thought I told Southern not to send me any more reps!"

"I'm Jenna. I'm here to apply for a hostess position," I said hesitantly. I handed him my resume, which I had worked on the night
before, making sure all my college honors were listed, as well as my
volunteer experience and past restaurant jobs.

Tony stopped then and looked me up and down. "What's your
name?" he asked again. He spoke with a thick Boston accent. He was
short and balding, with the authoritative air of an ex-police officer,
but he was dressed in board shorts and a faded T-shirt with surf-
boards on it.

"Jenna," I repeated. "I'm about to start culinary school down the
street, and I'm just looking for something about sixteen hours a week."

Tony stared at me and took a long sip of his coffee. "You're going
to school to be a chef but you want to work as a hostess? How about on
the line or back with the pastry girls?"

"Well . . ." I began, "I'm actually going to school to be a food writer,
not a chef. I want to write restaurant reviews and cookbooks and just
thought . . . "

Tony cut me off. "You work weekends?" he asked while scribbling
down notes on his yellow legal pad. Though I really wasn't thrilled
about the idea of working weekends, I knew he wouldn't hire me if I
said no.

"Yep. I'd prefer not to work Sundays, though, because I usually go
to church," I said. I hoped that Tony would at least grant me Sundays
free so I could drive home late Saturday night if I wanted to.

"Hmmmm . . . right. So you're a church girl, huh?" Tony looked
straight at me and raised his eyebrows. "Well, to be honest, I don't
really need any more part-time hostesses right now, especially those

that aren't one hundred percent available, but you've got a good resume, so I guess I'll give you a try. Just don't disappoint me." He told me that Tim, one of the managers, would be in touch, and I left the restaurant quickly, excited for my new job but at the same time intimidated and anxious.

When I got home, Helen was making goulash. Aromas of paprika and cooked meat filled the air, and my mouth began to water. "Well?" she asked. "How'd it go?" I pulled out the bar stool and sat down. "I got a job!" I said. "I'm not quite sure when I start, but they said one of the managers would be in touch."

"Hey, that's awesome! Congrats! I talked to my job, too; you'll never guess my hours!"

She told me they were starting her off with the all-night shift, meaning she'd just be getting back from work when I woke up for school in the morning. I had a feeling that our year wasn't going to be quite the crazy dream we had both envisioned a few months ago over lunch. I hated to think about Helen out there on the streets busting the bad guys—this was a girl who tried to save hurt animals when we were kids. Still, I knew I would support her and that we'd make the best of it.

A few days later, I started at Roy's. I made the rookie mistake of wearing my favorite black pumps and dress that first night, and spent the entire time in pain from the giant blisters that formed all over my heels. Tables constantly needing clearing, and families waited in line out the door to be seated. I quickly learned that succeeding in this job would require being good under pressure and being quick on my feet. The time I went home depended on how many tables were still occupied in the restaurant, but I could usually sweet-talk Tim into letting me head out after I seated the last one, rather than waiting for only three tables to be left like Tony made me do. On the average night, I usually took off around ten o'clock and tried to be asleep by eleven, so I could still manage six hours of rest before my alarm blasted at the crack of dawn. And, of course, right as my alarm was going off, Helen was pulling in from another long night at the police department.

The other two hostesses, Laura and Carol, became good friends of mine. Both were around my age and working their way through school like I was. Laura was pursuing her MBA at the University of Central Florida. She had been working at Roy's for three years and seemed to know all the restaurant's ins and outs. Carol, on the other hand, had been working at Roy's part-time for a year and a half to supplement the income she made at her nine-to-five job, which was in business development. Like Laura, Carol was sweet and genuine, and we could always make each other laugh. Right after I started, Carol surprised us all by getting married to a marine after a three-month whirlwind romance. As soon as I spotted her ring, a small but lovely diamond on her left hand, I gasped out loud because I knew Carol was as single as they come.

"What in the world is THAT?" I asked loudly one night, grabbing her hand, after we had worked together for a couple months.

Carol blushed bright red. "Well, I, um, got engaged! No one knows yet, though, so don't tell Tony. It's kind of a secret." Some secret, with her ring sparkling under the restaurant's bright lights.

"I had no idea you were even dating anyone . . . this is crazy! Congratulations!" I always loved hearing proposal stories and secretly wondered what and when my own would be. Carol's was extremely special though, and she recounted it to Laura and me one night after most of the tables in the restaurant were empty and things were winding down.

"It all happened about two months ago," she began, still blushing. "I was on my way home from Atlanta for a conference and was about to board my plane when I looked across the terminal and saw a really cute guy in a marine uniform. I know it sounds corny, but at that moment our eyes locked and I just knew! Both of our flights ended up being delayed, and when I was sitting in Starbucks he came and found me and we talked for about two hours. We exchanged numbers and email addresses, and when I finally got home that night I saw that he had already emailed me . . . and somehow it just went from there!" Laura and I were completely enthralled by her story and we ended up chatting about it until the time we clocked out and went home.

Kicked-up Turkey Meatloaf

Serves 6

Truth be told, I have never liked meatloaf. Until, that is, I tried making it with turkey instead of the traditional beef, pork, and veal mix. Mushrooms and lentils jazz things up a bit, and you'll love sandwiches made with leftovers the next day.

½ tablespoon olive oil
1 large onion, diced
1 large carrot, diced
2 cloves garlic, minced
2 cups mushrooms, chopped
1 cup cooked black or green lentils
1 teaspoon salt
¼ teaspoon freshly ground black pepper
1½ teaspoons Worcestershire sauce
¼ cup ketchup
¾ cup panko breadcrumbs
⅓ cup milk
1 pound lean ground turkey
1 egg, lightly beaten

For the glaze
2 tablespoons ketchup
1 tablespoon pure maple syrup
1 tablespoon balsamic vinegar

Preheat the oven to 400°F and grease a loaf pan.

In a large skillet, heat olive oil over medium-high heat until hot but not smoking. Add the diced onion and sauté until soft and translucent, about 6 minutes. Add the carrot and garlic and cook for 3 minutes. Add the chopped mushrooms and cook until all vegetables are softened, about 5 more minutes. Remove the pan from the heat and transfer the mixture to a large bowl. Add the cooked lentils, salt, pepper, Worcestershire sauce, and ketchup and mix well.

In a small bowl, combine the panko breadcrumbs and milk. Let sit for 3 minutes so the crumbs can absorb a little of the milk. Add to vegetable mixture.

Add ground turkey and beaten egg and mix well with your hands. Transfer to the loaf pan and press down to smooth top.

Combine the ingredients for the glaze and pour over top of meatloaf. Spread with a spoon to cover the top. Bake for 55 minutes or until a meat thermometer reads 165°F.

Homemade Baked Beans

Serves 2 hungry girls

This is, by far, one of the most praised recipes on my blog, and for good reason! Maple syrup, dry mustard, and hot sauce provide spicy sweetness for this country classic. For a meal in one dish, add hot chicken sausage to the beans before baking.

½ tablespoon extra-virgin olive oil
½ large yellow onion, chopped
3 cloves garlic, minced
8 ounces tomato sauce
2 tablespoons pure maple syrup
1 tablespoon ketchup
1 teaspoon dry mustard
1 teaspoon hot sauce
½ teaspoon sea salt
1 (15-ounce) can cannellini beans, drained and rinsed
1 bay leaf

Preheat the oven to 350°F.

In a cast-iron or nonstick skillet, heat the olive oil until hot but not smoking. Add the onions and sauté until soft and translucent, about 5 minutes. Add the garlic and sauté 30 seconds more.

Add the tomato sauce, maple syrup, ketchup, ground mustard, hot sauce, and sea salt, and simmer for 5 minutes.

Add the beans and bay leaf. Stir, then cover the skillet with aluminum foil and bake for 45 minutes, stirring halfway through the baking process.

Allow the beans to cool for about 10 minutes. Serve warm.

5

RUNNING ON EMPTY

AFTER ABOUT THREE WEEKS OF LIVING IN ORLANDO, I started to run. I figured that it was the best way to beat the "Cordon Bleu fifteen" that Rhonda had warned me about. Throughout my life, I'd never had a weight problem at all. I had been blessed with a good set of genes and simply never developed a taste for junk or fast food. I always preferred food that was as natural as possible, whether that came in the form of a creamy wedge of Brie or a perfectly ripe fig. I loved simple, honest food and believed everything could be enjoyed in moderation . . . especially rich, classic desserts. That being said, I still liked to take care of myself, and exercise had always played a very important role in my life.

So I invested in a good pair of sneakers and hit the pavement. My new apartment was conveniently located right next to the largest mall in Orlando, which provided an ample track to run around. Classes still hadn't started, and with my evening hours at Roy's, I had more than enough time to get moving in the morning. Truthfully, I never really enjoyed running as much as I enjoyed a sweaty yoga class, but I loved the feeling after a run when I made it into my apartment, cheeks red and sweat prickling my neck, to rummage through the cabinets for breakfast. I always ran slowly with my iPod on and usually stopped every few minutes for a short walk break.

Walking hindered my speed, of course, but it made the whole process more enjoyable.

I started running by myself because it wasn't really Helen's thing; plus we were operating on completely different schedules. Her hours ran her ragged until early in the morning, and sometimes she slept until two in the afternoon to make up for lost sleep. So I would sneak out quietly in the mornings, making sure to close the door softly and lock it on my way out. One morning, after my standard two-mile jog, I returned and found her sitting on the bar stool in her pajamas, eyes red and hair a sight.

"You look awful. Did everything go okay last night at work?" I asked as I took a long swig of cold water and then poured myself a cup of coffee.

"They tazed me," she said. "I knew it was coming, and it's just standard job training, but, man, did it ever hurt." Helen stuck out her right arm, which was now covered in angry red welts.

"Man, I'm so sorry. I guess you know how the bad guys feel now though, huh?"

Helen gave a dry laugh and drained her coffee cup. "This was bad, but it didn't hurt nearly as bad as when they maced me during initial training. Now that killed."

I gave her a sympathetic look, even though I had absolutely no idea how it felt to be tormented in that way. I still couldn't believe she was actually doing this. It just seemed . . . wrong.

"Anyway, my arm hurt so badly that I couldn't sleep and I was going to suggest going somewhere for breakfast, but when I woke up you had already gone on your run. I was too hungry to wait!"

"Aw, don't worry about it. I've gotta run to school soon anyway to pick up my knife set, so I'm a little short on time," I said as I opened the fridge to grab the low-fat milk and a bowl of fresh blackberries. Five minutes later, I was chowing down on a hot bowl of Scottish oatmeal, laced with honey and studded with the juicy berries. Helen had poured herself another cup of coffee and retreated to the couch, where she flipped on the Food Network. I kicked off my running shoes and thought about all I had to do that day to get ready for school.

After a few weeks, although I still didn't enjoy running, I felt myself get better at it, which I liked. My runs became part of my routine, and I found that after I ran, my days were always a little better and I slept deeper, too. On a whim, I decided to enter the Gasparilla Half Marathon four months later in Tampa. I'd never actually run a race before, but I liked the idea of having a goal in mind and something to train for while I cooked my days away in classroom kitchens. Even though I've always considered myself a spontaneous person, routine appealed to me, and I enjoyed having a plan and a schedule. I didn't know anyone else who was running the race, but I quickly found a training plan online that suited my frequent walk breaks and slower style. The plan had me increasing my mileage by one mile every week and incorporating cross-training, such as yoga.

By the third week of the new plan, though, my shins began to hurt. They started aching only a few minutes after I left the apartment, but usually got better toward the middle of my run. The pain was dull and annoying, and I started to apply ice packs after every run right as soon as I got back inside. I hated the ice and the way it felt like both shins were swollen and bruised deep within, but I still struggled to keep up with my training. On one particular 5-mile run, the pain became so sharp and strong that I actually had to stop and walk back. I decided to take two weeks off and wore Ace bandages and Tiger Balm pads on my shins, underneath my chef pants, when I was at school. I never saw a doctor, but I read online that the best thing to do was apply ice twice a day, every day. I iced three times a day because I was on my feet all day and all night between school and work, and I figured a little extra treatment couldn't hurt.

Two weeks later, I laced up my running shoes again, this time with a tight Ace bandage on my right shin and an ibuprofen already in my system. I opened my apartment door and felt a shock of cool late-October air as I warmed up and stretched. It was 6:30 in the morning, and the city was still very much asleep, with the exception of the bright lights moving on the interstate behind the apartment. I walked out of my complex and turned my walk into a slow jog as I headed to my usual around-the-mall loop. Not even five minutes later, my right shin felt like it was pulsating beneath the bandage. The pain made me angry, and I gritted my teeth and pushed myself forward, trying to focus on what I would be cooking later that day or the ingredients in a new pasta dish I wanted to test out. *Milk, tarragon, garlic, shallots, ooooouch!* I cursed silently, slowing my jog to a walk. I had put time, effort, and money into training for this race, and even though it hurt, I really didn't want to quit. *Plenty of people run with ailments*, I told myself. *Don't be such a wuss. Think of something nice . . . like bread or dark chocolate or baked feta cheese. This too shall pass.*

I picked up my speed and continued around the mall, the sun slowly starting to turn orange in the sky and mall employees emerging from their parked cars with hot coffees in their hands. I glanced down at my heart-rate monitor watch, which also tracked my distance. One point seven five miles, it blinked. *One point seven five?* I felt like I had been going now for at least three. My leg hurt and my mind started spinning. Why was I doing this anyway? I never really liked running to begin with, and there were plenty of other ways I could stay in shape without joining a gym, like power yoga and long walks. I thought of the hot coffee bubbling in the machine back at the apartment and the creamy Greek yogurt and homemade granola that would serve as my finishing prize. *Okay, Jenna . . . 4 miles left. You can do this . . . it's nothing!* With my mind made up, I pushed away all thoughts of my aching shin and my eventual breakfast and set my full attention on the road before me.

What felt like hours later, I returned to my front door, huffing and puffing with a shiny new blister poking out of my heel. Later that week, after spending a little more time online researching shin splints, I decided to seek out a special foot doctor who could maybe give me some professional training advice. Both Helen and Rob thought I was completely crazy to keep on running when it caused me so much pain, and I was beginning to feel the same way. I hoped that this new doctor could shed some light on the situation.

"Miss Weber, you have two options," Dr. Richards said, as I sat on the wrinkled white paper that covered the exam table. "Stop running, or learn to run through the pain. The pain isn't going to kill you, and there's only a very slim chance it will actually cause something more serious, like a stress fracture."

I just stared at him. "You mean . . . just run through it? Run through the pain? That's the answer?" I'd thought he was going to tell me about some treatment or low-cost therapy program that would diminish the pain.

"Yep. If you want. It's up to you. After looking at these X-rays and measuring your feet, I can see exactly what your problem is: your hips are off balance. This is causing more stress to be put on the right foot and, thus, giving you shin splits. There's really nothing we can do except prescribe you some orthotics that may or may not work. The best advice I can give you, as both a doctor and a fellow runner, is that you should keep at it. There might be pain, but you're an athlete and athletes deal with pain."

This was definitely not the answer I was hoping for. An athlete? Sure, I was training for a race, but I never actually considered myself an athlete. I was a cook and a wannabe food writer. I chopped chicken, sautéed garlic and, in my spare time, wrote poems. I wasn't an athlete by any stretch.

"Okay . . . well, thanks anyway. Hopefully it'll get better . . . ." I said, leaving the office in a hurry and calling Rob on my way out.

"He said to run through it! Run through the pain!! That's ridiculous!" I said angrily into the phone as I searched for my car in the doctor's parking lot.

"He said what? That's stupid, Jenna. I don't care what that quack says; you're really going to hurt yourself long term if you keep running like that. I can't believe he actually said that!"

I balanced the phone against my shoulder, fastened my seatbelt, and started the car, letting the air conditioning blast on my face to calm me down. "I mean . . . I don't want to quit, you know? I don't know . . . I guess I'll just see how it goes. I have to go—I'll call you later!"

I clicked my phone shut and started to think. Was the race really worth it? Was running even really worth it? If I didn't run, I'd probably have to spend at least fifty bucks a month joining a gym or doing more yoga classes, but then at least I wouldn't always be in pain. Still, part of me wanted to just finish what I started. It might hurt, but at least I wouldn't be a quitter.

I took three days off and then hit the pavement again. Afterward, it hurt to walk, and in the middle of the night when I got up to use the bathroom, I almost fell over. I hated the way my body felt weak and incapable. Finally, on yet another five-mile run, I called it quits. As much as I hated to admit it, there was no way in the world I could run thirteen miles if I couldn't make it through five without throbbing pain. I stumbled back into the house, threw my shoes in the closet, and called Rob to tell him I was done.

"I honestly think you made the right decision," he said. "I mean, why cause yourself that amount of pain? It's just a race!"

I sighed. "Yeah, I know. I just wanted to do it to prove something to myself, I guess. Oh well . . . there's always yoga!" I laughed sarcastically.

"To be honest, I never really saw you as a runner anyway, Jenna. You're always on the go and running from one place to the next, between work, culinary school, and shuttling from one city to the other . . . but running races? It's never really seemed like you. Do something that makes you feel good inside *and* out—that's the Jenna I know!"

Rob was always good with the pep talks.

"Hmm, I kinda like that," I said. "I can still be a 'runner,' but not in the literal sense of the word. I'll just keep running around, and eating, and living!"

After hanging up the phone, I wandered into the kitchen. As much as I knew it was the right decision to stop training for the race, I still felt like I was letting myself down a little bit. I grabbed a potato from the pantry and started peeling it over the sink, preparing to make a potato pancake for breakfast. Once I had the potato all peeled and smooth, I cut it into two and started grating each half on my old box grater over a piece of wax paper. Then, I dumped the grated potato into a large metal bowl, added sea salt, pepper, and a beaten egg, and formed the blob into a large shaggy pancake that I seared in a hot skillet coated with vegetable oil. It smelled like French fries and made me remember all the times my mom made potato pancakes at home, topping them with a spoonful of chunky applesauce and serving them alongside grilled pork tenderloin.

"Mmm, what's that smell?" Helen asked as she came into the kitchen.

"I was craving potato pancakes for some reason," I replied. "Want half?"

"Yeah, if you don't mind! That looks awesome."

I sprinkled a little additional sea salt on the now crisped and browned pancake and handed Helen half on a plate. "Want applesauce?" I asked her as I opened the fridge and grabbed the jar of Musselman's.

"No thanks, I'm good." She took a bite and widened her eyes. "Yum! Jenna, this is delicious!"

I put a big spoonful of applesauce on top of my pancake and dug in as well, relishing the sweet and salty combination. For a moment, I forgot all about the stress of running and concentrated on what really mattered to me, which was food and cooking. I might never be a runner, but maybe I could be a real food writer someday with a little training.

Potato Pancake for the Blues

Makes one jumbo pancake

Best made and eaten while wearing fuzzy pajamas and slippers. Things just taste better that way.

1 large russet potato
½ teaspoon sea salt
¼ teaspoon ground black pepper
1 egg, lightly beaten
1 tablespoon canola oil for light frying
Applesauce or sour cream for topping

Peel the potato and grate using a box grater. Season with sea salt and pepper and add the beaten egg, mixing everything until well combined.

Heat the canola oil in a large cast-iron skillet over medium-high heat. When oil is sizzling, gently drop in the potato batter and fry until golden brown and crispy, about 3 minutes per side.

Remove and serve immediately with applesauce or sour cream (or both!), alongside pork or eggs.

Slow-Cooker Pulled Pork

Serves 6–8

Be sure to grab Lawry's Baja Chipotle Marinade for this slow-cooker classic. It lends a zesty spice that's irresistible! Leftovers can be kept in the fridge for up to four days.

**2 pounds pork shoulder (ask your butcher if you don't
　　see it on the shelf)**
1 teaspoon salt
1 teaspoon ground mustard
¼ teaspoon cayenne pepper
½ onion, chopped
½ bottle Lawry's Baja Chipotle Marinade
½ bottle of your favorite barbecue sauce

Rub the pork shoulder all over with the salt, ground mustard, and cayenne. In a heavy pan over medium-high heat, brown the shoulder on all sides. This should take about 10 minutes.

Remove shoulder from pan and place in a slow cooker. Add chopped onion and sauces. Turn slow cooker on high and cook the pork for 6–8 hours, until it falls apart easily when pierced with a fork.

Remove pork from slow cooker and shred with two forks. Spoon sauce over top and serve.

6

OUI, CHEF!

M
Y NERVES WERE ON FIRE. THE NIGHT BEFORE, I HAD assembled everything perfectly. I had ironed and starched my uniform, organized my knife kit, and trimmed my fingernails shorter than they had ever been before, getting every tiny bit of old polish off. After work, I had tried to fall right asleep but ended up lying in bed for two hours. When the alarm finally rang, bright and early at 6 a.m., I leaped out of bed, anxious nerves turning into excitement about the day to come.

I arrived at school thirty minutes early and took a deep breath as I entered the kitchen classroom for the first time. My primary thought was how cold the room was, and I nervously fiddled with my cravat (a necktie that's part of the traditional chef's uniform) to disguise my shaking hands. There were only a few other students in the kitchen, and I recognized the face of a girl who had been in orientation with me a couple of weeks before. She returned my nervous smile, and I grabbed a metal bar stool from the corner of the kitchen and took a seat next to her alongside the metal counter. Out of my bag, I pulled a brand-new notebook with neat, smooth pages. I couldn't believe that only a few months ago I had been sitting in a Victorian Literature class, preparing to take my final exam. The minutes ticked down, and even though the room was chilly, I felt a prickle of sweat start at the base of my neck, where my long hair was gathered and pulled into a hairnet-covered tight knot.

More students filled the room, most of them boys who looked to be about eighteen. Only three other girls entered the kitchen, and for a moment I wondered what in the world I was doing here, thinking about how I probably should have followed everyone else's advice and gotten a safe and comfortable job after college instead of putting myself in thousands of dollars of student debt. It was too late for that now, though, and at exactly 7:30 a.m., Chef Stein walked into the kitchen. "LINE UP!!" he barked and then turned and walked right back out of the room. I took a deep breath and followed the rest of my classmates out of the room, where we formed a line with our backs straight against the wall while Chef shook our hands and inspected us individually. Since my last name begins with W, I was at the end of the line and waited nervously for my turn. Finally, I moved forward.

"Good morning, Chef!" I said in an overexcited tone, shaking his hand. Whenever I get nervous I act way too enthusiastic. He scanned his roster and glanced up at me.

"Why are you here, Weber?"

I paused, then smiled, showing my teeth. "Well, you see, I just graduated from the College of Charleston with a degree in English. After college I went to Paris to study travel writing, and now I'm here to learn everything about food so I can make a career as a food writer!" The overeager tone got the best of me again. I wanted to run far, far away.

Chef just stared at me with a deadpan expression and then smirked. "I didn't ask for your entire life story. I just wanted to know why you're here. Weber, there's nothing I hate more than a good restaurant critic. Personally, I'd like to fry 'em all up for breakfast and then cut into them like strips of crispy bacon. That's how I feel about food critics and now that's how I feel about you, too. From now on I'm going to just refer to you as 'the enemy.' How do you feel about that, Weber?" How did I feel? I felt like I was about to lose my breakfast right there on the shiny linoleum floor, that's how I felt. Instead, I just mumbled something unrecognizable and then scurried back into the kitchen to begin my first day of school.

Later, as I stood with my future peers in a huddle around a long rectangular table in the chilly classroom kitchen listening to Chef Stein dictate, my anxious nerves returned.

"I'm not here to be your friend, buddy, or pal. The rules are written in your book, and if you don't respect them then I will fail you and you will go home, no questions asked. This is my house and you will listen to what I have to say."

Chef was an ex-marine with a passion for classical cooking and a very long list of things he thought were "disgusting," such as the microwave, the Food Network, all celebrities, chain restaurants, shortcuts to anything . . . the list could go on for days. He was a large man with hair buzzed short in typical military style. When he looked at you, it was as if his blue eyes pierced right through you, just challenging you to look away.

Every response we gave to him had to be a "YES, CHEF" or "NO, CHEF" in unison. The louder we were, the happier he was. "Sounding off," it was called. To someone with my mild-mannered Southern upbringing, shouting in class seemed intense and unnatural. I always hated to be yelled at.

The classroom kitchen was large, with a long row of commercial-grade stoves in the middle and two long wooden countertops on each side. There was nothing on the walls, not even a clock, which Chef said would be too much of a distraction. In the back of the kitchen there were two large stockpots—large enough for a small person to stand in—in which chicken and veal stock bubbled continuously all day long. I learned that every morning we were to get to class thirty minutes early to set up our individual work space with a cutting board, a sanitizing bucket, a waste bucket, two dishcloths, and our tool kit. Homework was mandatory and reviewed aloud every morning—and Chef loved to call on unsuspecting students whom he thought might not have finished their work.

Also every morning, students were to procure food from the Purchasing Department, set up Chef's demo (complete with peeled vegetables and tools), fill the industrial-size three-compartment sinks with water and sanitizer for dishwashing, and arrange our own *mise en place*, ingredients and tools, so that we wouldn't waste any time after the demo. Timing was everything here, and part of our daily homework was to complete "timelines" of the next day's recipe, including all tools, ingredients, and preparations used.

That first morning, we were each assigned a workstation along the two countertop rows. I found myself the only girl on my end of the counter, which wasn't surprising given the ratio of men to women in the class. The three guys surrounding me were all from Florida, too, and had just graduated from high school the previous spring. Their faces bore remnants of adolescent awkwardness, with fading acne scars and faint shadows of beards. Frank, Jim, and Diego were all

from the same town and constantly bantered about different girls they'd been with, or made racist jokes. When I introduced myself initially, Diego made a low-pitched whistle and said something in Spanish while elbowing Frank. Color rose in my cheeks, but I was determined to meet their gaze and not back down. The four of us were going to be working together for the next three weeks, after all.

On the second day, I felt a bit more prepared for lineup, but I was worried about my triple-rolled checkered chef's pants, knowing I should have spent the extra twenty bucks to get them hemmed. My scalp had already begun to itch under the hairnet and my white hat.

"Good morning, Chef," I said loudly as we shook hands. He just looked at me and wrote a note on his paper.

"Hands," he barked, gesturing for me to stick out my hands so he could inspect them for any sort of cut or dirt speck hidden under my now too-short fingernails. "Socks." I pulled up my pant leg to show short white socks. He made a clicking noise with his tongue. "Miss Weber, are your pants hemmed?" There was no point in lying to him because I could tell he already knew.

"No, Chef," I responded.

"They'd better be by tomorrow. Get in class."

And so it was. That evening, when I got home from school, I sat in my apartment staring at my bank account on my laptop screen, half a turkey and cheese sandwich next to me. Getting my pants hemmed would eat into my food budget for the month. *Screw it,* I muttered under my breath, and decided to just do it myself. In my closet, I found the small plastic sewing kit my mom had given me— the same sewing kit that had remained sealed for the past four years

because, despite my childhood prairie-girl phase, I hate sewing with a burning passion. I told myself it must be done, though, and after I poured myself a large glass of wine I sat down on the couch with the Food Network on and prepared to hem my first pair of pants.

I worked and worked at it, but my efforts were in vain: the stitches came out loose and loopy. I wondered briefly if I should pick them all out and start over, but then I glanced at my watch and saw that it was already ten o'clock. I set the pants aside, fell into bed, and dreamed of checkered pants and life-size sewing needles stitching up my legs.

By the third day, my class officially lost our only fifteen-minute break of the day because a girl showed up *thirty seconds* late. Now we went straight through the five hours with no stopping. I didn't mind this as much as my partners, who, along with the other smokers in the class, suffered greatly from nicotine withdrawal during stressful situations.

On my fifth day of Basic Skills, we made our first dish to be graded, pasta with sautéed vegetables and pesto sauce. As soon as Chef said "Go," I raced to my station and began work on supreming and zesting an orange, along with the various knife skills I had to demonstrate before I could even start on my pasta. To perfectly supreme an orange means to leave it bare and juicy, with no flecks of stringy white pith at all. Sweat trickled beneath my cravat and I fought back exhaustion. I was quickly discovering that culinary school was more than just frosting cupcakes, as I had envisioned it. I was under more stress now than I had been all four years of college combined. We had an hour and a half to complete everything, and the timer was ticking.

I took out my sharp paring knife and made clean, easy cuts down the segments of my orange. I wiggled each glistening segment out gently but still managed to lose half of each one. I scraped off every speck of pith, for if Chef saw any white at all we would lose points. In the end, I had no pith on my segments, but they were ugly and misshapen—not at all like the perfect ones that Chef had produced effortlessly in a matter of minutes during the demo. I took a deep breath, put the segments in a ramekin, with pretty ones on top to hide my mistakes, and began work on the other knife skills. While I was working, I glanced over at Frank's tray. I had to admit, for being crude and obnoxious, he was a pretty good chef. All of his oranges were perfectly supremed, and he chopped so fast it looked like his knife never left the cutting board. I quickly got back to my work.

I cut an onion the way Chef demonstrated—peeling it, slicing it in half, and then making vertical and horizontal cuts, leaving the root ends attached. This was supposed to produce perfect small dice, all uniform and complete. After chopping, though, I noticed that some of my dice were quite a bit larger than the others. With the clock ticking, I had no choice but to put them all in a ramekin and let them go. After my onion was chopped, my orange was supremed, and my shallot and garlic were minced until they were barely recognizable, I took my silver sheet pan and ramekins to the front to be graded.

"I'm finished, Chef," I said as I stood there, rather awkwardly, with my large tray held out before me.

Chef didn't say anything at first, just made a low grunting noise while he finished jotting something down in his book. Finally, he looked up. "Ah, the enemy," he said with a grin. "Let's see what you got, Weber."

Immediately he went straight for my misshapen oranges. "These are not how I demonstrated. See how yours falls apart when picked up? You were overzealous with your knife. Be gentle. I could not serve these." My cheeks began to burn, and I could only nod. He then picked at my onion dice, separating the good ones from the longer pieces. "These need to be uniform. All the same size, perfect quarter-inch dice. Every one of them. You need to throw away the ones that do not fit that mold." He marked some numbers in his grade book and looked up at me. "You better get going, Miss Weber."

I hustled off to start on my pasta. This had been the first real test of my culinary skills, and I felt like I had already failed. I had one hour left, and Chef had told us that on this day, about eighty-five percent of students get a zero for lack of finishing. Thirty minutes later, after my *torchon* (hand towel) almost caught fire on my gas burner, my onions hit the oil without any hiss of a sizzle, which meant the oil had not warmed up enough. I finished with only five minutes to spare, but at least I finished. I anxiously seasoned my pasta with salt and pepper and piled it into a large stainless-steel bowl before taking it up to Chef to taste and grade.

This time: "Not enough salt." He chewed on a diced vegetable. "Vegetables are cooked nicely, and so is the pasta, but there is not nearly enough salt in this . . . and a little too much oil." He gave me a four out of five as my final grade for the day and left me to pile my greasy, undersalted pasta into a Styrofoam cup to have for dinner that night at home. A lot of my classmates were still struggling with their sauté pans and water that was refusing to boil. I exhaled. One day down, fourteen more to go.

I ditched the pasta and came home that afternoon completely exhausted, bearing a couple of potatoes and leeks that Chef had given me to "practice" with. Helen was just waking up from a nap and laughed when she saw my arms full of dirty potatoes.

"More pancakes?" she asked.

I just gave her a glare. "Ugh, I wish. Chef is making me practice my knife skills with these . . . part of my 'homework.' I didn't do as well as I'd hoped on the first graded plate, so I guess this is the consequence."

"Well, at least we know we'll never go hungry!" Helen laughed. "Can we make mashed potatoes with the leftovers? I'm craving something creamy and comforting."

I nodded and immediately got to work, peeling the potatoes and slicing them directly down the middle to start and then into perfect medium-size dice according to Chef's instruction. "Honestly, it's not totally what I thought so far . . . but it's still fun," I said as I chopped. "I just want to get past all this initial stuff and move on to the fun, creative cooking."

"Yeah, but don't you have to be sure you know the basics before you can move on? It'll all pay off in the end," Helen replied. Cooking at home had already begun to take on a whole new meaning without Chef constantly in my ear and mind and without the classical music droning. Even my dreams at night were consumed with chopping and slicing, and at times I swore I could hear Chef shouting in the background. However, by the end of that first week my vegetable-dicing skills were almost professional and I was proud that my practice at home had really paid off.

Pasta with Sautéed Vegetables and Pesto

Serves 4

I love this tasty vegetarian pasta dish but have been known to add chicken sausage to kick it up a notch. During the summer, I make big batches of pesto and freeze it so that I can enjoy this dish whenever the mood strikes.

For the pesto
   3 cups packed basil leaves
   3 garlic cloves
   ½ cup extra-virgin olive oil, divided
   Juice of ½ lemon
   ¼ cup grated Parmesan cheese
   ½ teaspoon sea salt, or to taste
   ¼ teaspoon freshly ground black pepper, or to taste

For the pasta
   8 ounces dried bow-tie pasta
   1 tablespoon canola oil
   1 small summer squash, diced
   1 red bell pepper, diced
   1 yellow bell pepper, sliced
   Freshly grated Parmesan cheese to taste
   Freshly ground black pepper to taste

Make the pesto: Add the basil, garlic, and 2 tablespoons of the oil to a high-speed blender or food processor and blend on high until smooth. With the blender on low speed, slowly add the remaining oil in a stream, then add the lemon juice and cheese and continue blending until smooth. Transfer the pesto to a bowl and add the salt and pepper.

Make the pasta: Cook the pasta in a pot of boiling salt water until *al dente*, then drain and set aside. Dry the pot and return it to the stovetop. Heat the oil in the pot over medium-high heat until hot but not smoking then add the squash and bell peppers and cook, stirring, until just tender, about 5 minutes.

Add the pasta with about ½ cup of the pesto, or to taste, to the pot with the sautéed vegetables and toss to combine. Sprinkle with the freshly grated Parmesan cheese and black pepper and serve.

Spicy Roasted Root Vegetables

Serves 4

Aside from being a great way to practice your knife skills, this side dish is easy and delicious. Sweet potatoes or butternut squash make nice additions when they are available.

2 carrots, peeled and diced
1 rutabaga, peeled and diced
1 turnip, peeled and diced
1 large parsnip, peeled and diced
Splash of olive oil
4 tablespoons minced parsley
Sea salt and pepper to taste
Cayenne pepper to taste

Preheat oven to 400°F. Keep all medium-size diced vegetables separate in little piles or bowls. Combine the carrots and rutabaga in a roasting pan. Roast for 5 minutes. Add the turnip and parsnips, drizzle with oil, and continue to roast until tender, about 5 more minutes. When the vegetables are tender, remove from oven, sprinkle with parsley, and season with salt and cayenne pepper.

Chicken-Pepperoni Parmesan

Serves 4

This is a great way to jazz up traditional Chicken Parmesan. Serve with spaghetti and additional sauce on the side.

- 2 eggs
- ¼ cup milk
- 2 cups panko breadcrumbs
- ½ cup flour
- 4 chicken breast halves, pounded thin
- Salt and pepper to taste
- 2 tablespoons canola oil
- 1 large jar marinara sauce
- ¼ cup freshly grated Parmesan cheese
- 1 cup shredded mozzarella
- 2 ounces pepperoni (I use turkey pepperoni)

Preheat the oven to 450°F.

In a shallow dish or pie plate, combine eggs and milk. Put panko in another shallow dish, and spread out flour in a third shallow dish.

Season chicken with salt and pepper. Batter one breast at a time by dunking it in the egg-milk mixture, then the flour and finally the panko. Repeat until all chicken breast halves have been covered with batter.

In a large ovenproof skillet over medium heat, heat canola oil until shimmering. Add the chicken breasts and lightly fry until golden on both sides and cooked through, about 8 minutes.

Cover with marinara sauce, Parmesan, and mozzarella. Finally, lay the pepperoni slices on top.

Transfer the skillet to the oven and bake for 15 minutes.

7

MAKE THEM FEEL
LIKE YOU CARE

I WAS DUE IN TO THE RESTAURANT AT FOUR O'CLOCK AND probably wouldn't get off until close to eleven, seeing as it was Friday night, the busiest night of the week at Roy's. On the kitchen counter were stacks of my notes from class, recipes for chicken stock and béchamel sauce, grease stains on the edges. I pushed them aside and wrote a quick note to Helen that I had some pasta primavera leftovers in the fridge from class and that I would probably be home late. Then, I untied my sneakers, flung them across the room, and hopped in the shower. I had a fresh burn on the inside of my right wrist, an unfortunate result of letting the tender skin touch a five hundred–degree sheet pan full of Parmesan *tuiles* straight from the oven. The hot shower burned my blistery skin, and I held up my arm to shield it. Once upon a time, I had unblemished skin and manicured nails. Now my arms more resembled a line cook's and my fingernails those of a dishwasher. I didn't really mind, though, other than when I got odd stares and glances at the restaurant. I gathered people thought I had a cutting problem, which always made for interesting conversation.

After my shower, I pulled on my standard work outfit—a black A-line skirt, black sweater, and heels. It felt so odd to wear nice clothes after running around in baggy checkered pants and an oversized chef jacket all day. I felt like I was constantly playing two parts, with one foot still in the world of heels and pearls, and the other in that of grease and frying pans. I got to work early, as usual, so that I could pick up some tea from the Starbucks next door to sip at the hostess stand. As I walked through the restaurant doors, Laura immediately looked up and gave me a big, warm smile.

I noticed the restaurant was just starting to fill up for the night; it was mostly families with small children occupying the roomy booths along the wall.

"How are you, Laura?" I asked her while setting my purse down below the stand.

"Good. Tonight should be a busy one," she said. "We have about 140 on the books with mostly late reservations." She made a face. We both hated late reservations because the later people sat down to eat, the later we had to stay. I took my stand next to her and started preparing special birthday menus with pieces of colorful ribbon tucked inside. It was only 5:30, and we had about an hour until things really started to pick up.

Just then, Tony walked out from the back office. The look on his face told me he was in another one of his classic moods, and more than anything I just wanted to stay out of his way. He walked right up to the hostess stand and stared at the computer for a moment.

"Girls, the Greens are coming in tonight, and they had a really bad experience last time. I want both of you to make tonight the best night of their damn life, you hear me?" Tony was talking to both of us, but he was looking straight at me and just his presence almost made me start to sweat.

"Of course, Tony," Laura said. "They're coming in at eight, so I'll set their table up early with some Hawaiian flowers and a candle."

"Nice, Laura. Now you," he said, pointing at me. "You need to start being more assertive with guests. Have conversations with them, get to know their babies, that kind of stuff. Make them feel like you care about them. That's how people feel special and then want to come back. Don't just stand up here like a stone. Do something with yourself!"

I could feel my face start to burn. I had always been introverted, and there was nothing I hated more than confrontation. "Of course," I said. "I'm sorry; I'll really try to do better."

Tony stared at me for a second and then walked away without another word.

"I know he seems hard, but I promise he's like a teddy bear deep down," Laura said sympathetically. "It took him forever to warm up to me, too. That's totally normal."

"I hope so," I said. "Between him and my chef-instructors at school, I constantly feel like I'm up in arms."

"Seriously . . . I don't think Tony started liking me at all until I had worked here for a year. Before that he just thought I was some airhead, I think. I had to prove myself to him first by putting in the time here." Laura shrugged. "Now he's almost like my second dad or something. I know he'd help me out in any situation."

"Well, you're lucky then. I still think he thinks I'm a dumb blonde," I said right as the double doors swung open and a family of eight walked in.

"Aloha!" Laura called out and I started to prepare four children's menus with crayons. It was 6:45 now, and the rush was about to begin full-force. I was glad I'd packed a gingerbread cookie in my purse for later because I had a feeling I would need it. The cookie was from my favorite bakery in Tampa; I had picked up a few when I went home last weekend, and had hoarded them like gold ever since. The thick, spicy cookie was one of the best I had ever eaten, and though I'd tried numerous times, I had never been able to make my own as well as the bakery could.

Around 9 p.m. the restaurant was still jam-packed. In an effort to please Tony, I had thrown myself into making absolutely sure the Greens had a wonderful dining experience; I had even stopped to chat at several other tables. Tony was in the back, shouting at the line cooks. He had sweat dripping off his bright red face and was throwing his hands around violently. I stood up at the hostess stand, sneaking bites of gingerbread cookie from my purse, and smiled to myself. Despite Tony and his crazy mannerisms, I still loved the intense atmosphere of the restaurant.

A few of the cooks knew I was going to LCB, and one was even in my program. They had questioned me early on as to why I didn't want to work in the kitchen with them, why I'd settled for a lowly front-of-house position. I just smiled and said it was temporary and this was what worked with my schedule. The real reason, though, was that the idea of working in the kitchen scared the heck out me. Working in a classroom kitchen under a chef-instructor's supervision was one thing, but the thought of working on the line, making people's dinners as quickly as I could, made me want to crawl into a hole and hide. I suppose that's why I went into my program with the firm knowledge that I wanted to write about food rather than cook it. Writing was safe.

I could hide behind my laptop and dodge the grease, the yelling, and the pressure that the kitchen brought every night. When you worked on the line, it almost seemed like you were on the front lines every single day. My quiet, conservative demeanor didn't seem to fit with the back of the house, and I was fine with that, though it was always a topic of conversation with my peers at school.

"Weber! What are you doing just standing there?" Suddenly Tony was behind me, and I could feel his hot breath on the back of neck.

"I just got through booking some new Christmas Eve reservations," I said. "I'm sorry."

"I hired you to work, not just to stand there and look pretty," he replied. "If you don't have anything to do, you can go help Jason clear some tables. If you haven't noticed, we're slammed." Tony's voice offered no room for discussion, and I gritted my teeth and smiled.

"Sure," I said. I left the stand and made my rounds, picking up napkins, stacking dirty plates, and gathering silverware. Laura had been allowed to go home early, so it was just me now. I glanced at my watch and checked my phone for text messages. Finally, an hour later, the last of the tables was leaving and I wandered to the back, looking for a manager to ask if I could head out for the evening. As I walked back to the office, I heard laughter coming from the kitchen and glanced up to see Tony with his son on his shoulders, joking with the chef. The little boy was all smiles and was hugging Tony's neck for dear life.

So maybe he does have a soft side, I thought to myself. Laura had said that more than anything Tony loved kids, and that's why Roy's was so child friendly. We kept a big cabinet full of toys, games, and pillows up front near the hostess stand, and I had seen Tony playing with the children before. It was as if kids were the crack in his "mean-guy" façade, and I had to admit, he wasn't so intimidating with a cute little boy on his back.

Tony saw me standing near the office and called over to me. "How'd it go, Weber?" he asked in a much friendlier voice than before.

I smiled. "It was a good night. Busy, but everyone seemed happy, and the Greens seemed to have a wonderful time."

"Good," Tony said. "Thanks for all your hard work tonight. I know your schedule is tight right now, but thanks for being here. You can go." He turned his back and then returned to laughing with his son, leaving me standing there with my mouth wide open.

A compliment from Tony? That had surely never happened before. After his hard words earlier in the night, I was convinced that he hated me. Now, the simplest of compliments completely made my night, and I smiled broadly while I walked back through the restaurant, out the door, and to my car. When I got back to the apartment, Helen was heating up some chicken soup in the microwave.

"Hey, stranger!" she said. We really hadn't seen much of each other lately, with my busy school and work schedule and her odd hours. She had dark circles around her eyes and looked like she had lost a little bit of weight off of her already very slender frame. I set my bag down on the counter and pulled up a bar stool.

"How are you? How's work?" I asked her.

"It's okay . . . not exactly how I pictured it going, but that's life, you know?" Helen's words were soft and hinted there was more to the story.

"I can't even imagine. I feel like all I do is complain about my busy schedule, but you're over here hardly sleeping and potentially getting shot at!" I laughed to lighten the mood.

Helen smiled. "Well, I don't know about all of that. It's just hard. The only other girl in my department quit today, so now I feel like I'm all alone with all the guys. I want them to treat me the same as they would each other, but it's difficult."

"I know exactly what you mean," I said. "I know it's a totally different scenario, but there are hardly any girls in my program, either. All day long I deal with dirty jokes and adolescent boys staring at my boobs."

Helen finished her soup by the sink and ran some water in her bowl before placing it in the dishwasher. "Yeah . . . some days I just wonder if I made the right decision doing this. I could be halfway through fashion school by now!"

To me, Helen had always seemed much more the fashion-designer type, but she was hell-bent on catching the bad guys.

"You could always play the 'what-if' game," I said. "I do the same thing. If I weren't here right now, I'm sure I would be living in Tampa and working some nine-to-five starter job at a PR agency or something. This is hard, but it's much more interesting!"

Helen nodded. "Yeah, you're right. I'm sure it will get easier. I'm going to head to bed—I have a long day tomorrow and feel like I haven't slept in weeks."

I said goodnight and headed into my room for bed as well. Every night when I got home from work, my favorite thing to do was run a hot bubble bath and soak my aching feet for a few minutes. Sometimes

I read in the bath, but other times I just zoned out, letting my mind wander away from meat temperatures and kitchen-safety regulations for a little while. What would I be doing if I weren't here right now? It all seemed to work out so perfectly, with her moving here and finding the apartment so quickly. I loved school, for the most part, and was glad that I'd made the decision to move here, but it was always interesting to think just how different life could be as the result of one decision.

Old-Fashioned Gingerbread Cookies

Makes about 4 dozen large gingerbread men

If you enjoy gingerbread cookies as much as I do, you really should try this recipe for a thick, moist, and chewy version. To make gingerbread cookie sandwiches, cut cookie dough in 4-inch circles and sandwich the cookies together with Chocolate-Buttercream Frosting (p. 15).

- ⅔ cup packed dark brown sugar
- ⅔ cup molasses
- 1 teaspoon cinnamon
- 1 tablespoon ground ginger
- ½ teaspoon ground cloves
- ¼ teaspoon ground white pepper
- 2 teaspoon baking soda
- 2 sticks (½ pound) unsalted butter, cut into pieces
- 1 egg, lightly beaten
- 3¾ cups all-purpose flour
- ½ teaspoon salt

Preheat the oven to 325°F.

In a large heavy-bottom pot, combine brown sugar, molasses, cinnamon, ginger, cloves, and white pepper. Bring to a boil over high heat and continue to boil for about 3 minutes, stirring occasionally.

Remove pot from stove and add baking soda, stirring to combine well (be careful: the mixture will bubble up here—just keep stirring!). Add butter a few chunks at a time, stirring to combine with each addition. Add egg and stir. Stir in the flour and salt gradually. The dough will be very soft and still warm.

Roll out the dough ¼-inch thick on a floured surface and cut it into rounds with a cookie cutter or large glass.

Bake cookies, spaced 2 inches apart, until golden and just set, about 12 minutes. Transfer to wire racks to cool. The cookies will firm up as they cool.

8
KNIVES OUT

AS I STEPPED INTO MEAT FABRICATION CLASS ON THE FIRST day, there was only one sound to be heard: the slamming of frozen meat on stainless-steel counters. The kitchen was cold enough to take my breath away. As I walked in and took my seat, I glanced up at the thermostat on the wall and saw that the temperature read fifty-two degrees. The assistant chef, a small woman who appeared to be in her late twenties, saw me looking. "Gotta keep it cold so the meat stays fresh," she said. "You'll learn to wear layers in here." I nodded and crossed my arms for warmth. The chef coat that once felt thick and heavy on me now felt like a layer of sheer cotton.

"Girl, you gotta dress warmer! It's only going to get colder in here once Chef starts pulling out the meat!" said the girl who was sitting across from me at the counter. She rolled up the sleeves of her coat to reveal another layer of cotton. "The secret is these little boys' long underwear from Walmart. Got a four-pack for only five dollars last weekend, and they pretty much fix the problem." She laughed and her eyes twinkled.

"I'll have to remember that! I'm always cold anyway, but this is brutal. I'm Jenna, by the way." I extended my hand to her as the other students started to pour in the kitchen now, most of them making jokes about the temperature as well.

"I'm Cat. This is my second time taking Meat Fab, so I know the drill. Seriously, get yourself to Walmart, or just start eating more of what we're cooking—you're a skinny one!" Cat laughed again, and I had a feeling we would get along just fine. Coming from Basic Skills, where I had been surrounded by adolescent boys all day every day, laughing with another girl came as a welcome relief. Diego and Frank were in the class, too, but we were no longer bound as partners and they had formed their own guys-only group on the other side of the kitchen. Despite our having formed an odd friendship toward the end of Basic Skills, I didn't really miss them too much. Just then, Frank looked over in my direction and waved, and I smiled.

Only a few minutes later, we headed back outside the kitchen for lineup, which felt like second nature to me now. Some of the students in line had been in my previous class, but I noticed quickly that a handful had dropped out, mainly girls. A few people I didn't recognize at all, and wondered if they, like Cat, were taking the class for the second time. We had two chefs for this class, Chef Sharmin and Chef Zoey, who had spoken to me earlier regarding the temperature in the kitchen. Chef Sharmin was a tall, lanky man who looked to be in his early forties.

"Miss Weber," he said in a nasally voice when it was my turn in line.

"Good morning, Chef Sharmin. It's nice to meet you," I replied as I routinely stuck out my hands to him so he could inspect my nails.

"You're pretty skinny," Chef said. "I hope you're not one of those vegetarian types." He sniffed his nose and raised his eyes to me.

I silently thanked God that I *wasn't* one of those vegetarian types anymore. While in college, I had dabbled in vegetarianism for a year, but a delicious *croque monsieur* in Paris the previous summer changed my diet forever. After one bite of that grilled ham and cheese sandwich, I knew I could never turn back.

"No, sir. I love meat," I said.

Chef looked hard at me. "Good. Because I fail vegetarians. Now get in the kitchen."

That morning we got lectured about how we weren't at Le Cordon Bleu to learn the art of making salads and grilled cheese, we were there to perfect classical French culinary techniques. Chef went on to tell us that we were expected to taste every single thing that was prepared in the class. No rule said we had to like it, but we had to at least try it all. Our syllabus featured conventional meats such as chicken, pork, and beef but also included rabbit, alligator, frog, and oxtail. My stomach churned at the very thought of eating an actual tail, and again I was thankful that I had left my vegetarian ways behind somewhere on the Left Bank in Paris.

I quickly decided I liked Chef Zoey much better than Chef Sharmin. For starters, she was a woman, and that alone was a rarity in the kitchen. She was short and muscular, no doubt from heaving heavy pots of stock around the kitchen, and wore her light brown hair in a short, bouncy ponytail beneath her tall chef's hat. When Chef Zoey spoke, she spoke with authority, daring any of the snarky teenage boys in class to give her attitude.

As both chefs continued to lecture, I learned that during the course of three weeks, I would memorize every part of a cow and pig and the slaughtering process that brought the steak to the table. Some of the dishes we were to make sounded delicious, such as pulled pork with Texas coffee barbecue sauce, perfect roast chicken, and beef stew.

Pulled pork was a dish I had discovered after my vegetarian stint, and now I couldn't get enough. I loved the tangy vinegar-based sauce local to South Carolina, where I went to college, and couldn't wait to learn how to make it myself. I figured the skill would come in handy for tailgating and football games, something Rob would love as well.

Later that morning we were again assigned groups for the rest of the three weeks, and unfortunately I was not with my friend Cat. Instead, I found myself again in a group with two guys, though this time they were my age and seemed a little more serious than Frank and Diego. Our first assignment was oxtails, and if you have never prepared oxtails before, I don't recommend it. Eating all parts of the animal may be a status symbol in certain foodie circles, but the minute the box of tails was set down in front of us, I felt nauseated. The tails were pasty white and looked like pure fat globbed on Popsicle sticks.

I reached hesitantly into the cardboard box and picked up a stick with a gloved hand. Chef had demonstrated how we were to slice off extra fat from the tail, leaving only a small amount of meat to be consumed. I picked up my paring knife and gently ran the edge of it down the tail, scraping off a thick layer of gelatinous fat with it. Carlo and Josh, my two new partners, laughed and joked in Spanish as they, too, scraped their oxtails.

I stood with one hand clutching the tail and the other holding the laminated recipe, as I tried to figure out what the next step was.

"So, I think we just get as much fat as we can off the tails and then sear them in oil before braising," I said. I couldn't imagine actually eating this dish, which still seemed to be pure fat despite my desperate attempts to scrape the tail.

"This is a traditional dish where I come from," Carlo said. "We usually serve it only on Christmas, though, 'cause it's so rich."

Rich is right! I thought, and proceeded to heat the oil and drop in the tails one by one. They sizzled when they hit the hot fat and smelled almost like burgers. Soon, the tails grew golden brown and the fat pooled around them in glistening puddles. While I had been working on the tails, Josh had put together a mix of sautéed *mirepoix* (onion, carrot, and celery) and deglazed the pan with some white wine and chicken stock. I carefully transferred the sizzling tails to the other pan, and Carlo quickly poured more stock on top.

"There!" I said. "I guess that needs about an hour to cook, so we can get all our cleanup done early." Other students were still searing their tails and chopping onions, and I felt very glad for my fast little group. The guys went outside for their cigarette break and I started scrubbing the table. I had to admit that the oxtails smelled a lot better now, simmering with rich stock and vegetables, than they had on their own. I peeked under the lid and saw white foam dotting the top of the stock; carrots rose and fell in the bubbles.

When it was finally done and we came together as a class to taste the fruits of our labor, I brought a spoonful to my lips and paused. The cooked tails still smelled vaguely like hamburgers, and tiny bits of meat and fat had fallen off the tail and now swirled in the stew as well. It looked good. I put the spoon in my mouth and chewed. I had to admit, the flavor wasn't all bad, but the texture of the tail was what got me. It really was just like a fat-covered Popsicle, and the meat felt stringy and greasy in my mouth. I set the bowl down and took a sip of water. At least I had tasted it.

Over the next three weeks, I worked harder than I ever had for anything in my life. I cut, butchered, and seared. I memorized all the parts of a cow and pig, and scared Helen half to death in the kitchen one night as I practiced deboning a chicken while in my pajamas around midnight. I had only a few days until my final practical for the class, where we would have to break down both a chicken and a fish completely, each in less than two minutes. *Breaking down* was a term used to describe the process of turning the animal from a whole carcass into edible portions. We were expected to know the different bones and how to remove them gently, with swift slits of the knife, so as to not tear the gentle flesh. Everything needed to be intact, clean, and ready to throw in a hot skillet.

Despite my hard work, I was worried about the final, mainly because my heart just wasn't in cutting up animals. I liked to eat meat, but butchery wasn't for me. At home, I preferred to cook simple meals like pasta or vegetables, foods that didn't have eyes and feelings. On the wall in the classroom kitchen, a huge framed poster of the different parts of the pig stared back at me, and I couldn't help but wonder what animals really thought as they were led into the slaughterhouse.

I knew that because I wasn't giving it my all, my grades were suffering. The next day, Chef Sharmin called me into his office. While I sat there shivering in my long underwear under my whites, he told me that I wasn't "putting maximum effort into the class" and that I needed to start "acting more like a real chef and less like a little girl." I felt tears start to sting my eyes and bit my bottom lip hard. As Chef added that my grade in this class depended on the final practical exam, I stared at my cuticles.

"You got it, Miss Weber? Go home tonight and practice. I want one hundred percent tomorrow morning, or else."

"Thanks, Chef. I got it. I really have been practicing at home, though, I swear. It just doesn't come easy to me, that's all." I thought back about deboning a chicken last night at midnight. And for what? Apparently Chef still thought I didn't deserve to be here in the first place.

The next morning, I was feeling surprisingly well rested and ready to roll. We were to start with the chicken, then move on to the fish. "Knives out . . . and GO!" yelled Chef Zoey. The chatter in the room vanished, and now all you could hear was the slicing of raw meat, tendons, and gristle. I mentally told myself to slow down and concentrate, trying to envision my diagram with all the correct knife cuts.

I made my first slice right underneath the gelatinous layer of cold skin on the top of the bird, so that I could slowly peel it away and get to work on the meat. Then, I cut deep down the center, along the top of the breastbone. I used my freshly sharpened paring knife to cut two even slits on the side of each breast, then ran my knife once again underneath each to totally remove them from the body. Feeling better that the initial slices were done, I laid both breasts, smooth side up, on the platter that I would later present to the chefs. I tried to imagine that I was back in my kitchen at home and that this wasn't for a grade but only for a dinner that would taste amazing. I then slit the connections between the legs and the wings, feeling a little resistance under my knife. After I heard the familiar snap of the tendon that connected the wings, I was able to separate wing from thigh and use the edge of my knife to saw away all the wing meat. Finally, I sliced off both thighs and pulled out the wishbone. I was done with part one.

My knife was covered with bits of chicken fat and meat. I wiped it clean with my towel, then dipped it quickly into the bowl of sanitizer on the table while I looked around to see Carlo and Josh's progress. They both had finished their chickens and started on the fish, which was definitely the harder of the two animals to break down completely. I glanced around at the rest of the class and noticed that one guy, an old cook from a navy ship with a don't-mess-with-me attitude, had finished both pieces completely and now raced outside for a cigarette break. I went to the walk-in fridge and picked one of the few remaining fish. It had a bulging eye that stared at me from the bottom of the cooler. Back at my station, I held my breath and cut off the head aggressively, suddenly hating this fish and this class and wondering what in the world I was actually doing here. Midway through removing the miniscule pin bones that ran down the center of each opaque fillet, I felt like something was going wrong. I had managed to slice out both fillets, but in attempting to rid them of all bones, I'd mangled them pretty badly. I had a smear of fish guts on my starched white apron and scales wedged underneath my fingernails.

When it was finally my turn in line to present what I had done, I showed off my chicken first. I was pretty proud of it, although I certainly wasn't to the point of considering a career in animal butchery any time soon.

"Nice work on the chicken, Weber, but what in the world happened to the fish?" Chef Sharmin sniffed and looked me straight in the eyes.

"Yeah, I'm not sure what happened there. Maybe my knife wasn't sharp enough . . . " I trailed off because I knew there was nothing I could say to remedy the situation, and if I kept talking I would probably only make things worse. Chef shook his head and scribbled some numbers down in his grade book, then waved his hand to tell me he was through with me.

"Thank you, Chef," I said and then washed my hands, hung up my apron, and stepped out of the kitchen to take a breather before the traditional "post-practical deep clean" began.

For the rest of the day, I kept finding the occasional fish scale stuck to my shoe or forearm. In the end, I managed to scrape by with a B– in the class. If I had perfected the fish the grade probably would have been higher, but I took what I could get.

Croque Monsieur

Serves 2

I like my croque monsieurs sans traditional béchamel sauce. For me, the sauce distracts from the delicious simplicity of the sandwich. Instead, I love to slather mine with Dijon mustard. Another fabulous variation is the croque madame, which is simply a croque monsieur with a fried egg on top.

**4 slices white sandwich bread (preferably a day old),
    crusts removed
Dijon mustard
8 ounces freshly grated Gruyère cheese
2 ounces country-style ham or Virginia ham,
    sliced moderately thin**

Preheat oven to 400°F.

Toast bread slices lightly in the oven. Lightly brush one side of each slice with mustard, then add cheese to two slices and add ham to the remaining two. Sandwich the ham and cheese parts together and bake until cheese melts, about 5 minutes.

Lemon–Brown Sugar Chicken

Serves 4

I just love this simple chicken dish—the perfect combination of sweet and sour! Serve it with roasted Brussels sprouts and a baked sweet potato for a complete meal.

1 pound boneless, skinless chicken breast
1 cup lemon juice
1 cup flour
1 teaspoon salt
1 teaspoon paprika
Dash of freshly ground black pepper
2 tablespoons canola oil
2 tablespoons chicken stock (recipe follows)
2 tablespoons brown sugar
1 tablespoon grated lemon zest

Combine chicken and lemon juice in a bowl and marinate in refrigerator for at least 30 minutes and up to 8 hours.

Drain the chicken and set aside. Fill a plastic bag with flour, salt, paprika, and pepper. Shake well. Add the chicken and shake to coat completely.

Heat canola oil in a large skillet (preferably cast iron) until hot but not smoking. Add the chicken and cook about 6 minutes on each side, until browned. Remove chicken from pan and deglaze with stock. Return chicken to pan.

Sprinkle the brown sugar and lemon zest over chicken and transfer to oven to finish baking, about 30 minutes.

Spicy Chicken Tortilla Soup

Serves 6

Serve this with lots of shredded Monterey Jack cheese, sliced jalapeños, and cornbread on the side for the perfect belly-warming meal that heals just about anything.

- 1½ pounds boneless skinless chicken breasts
- 1 poblano pepper
- 2 tablespoons olive oil
- 1 large red onion, diced
- 1 jalapeño pepper, diced (include seeds, if desired)
- 2 cloves garlic, minced
- 2 teaspoons chili powder
- 2 teaspoons cumin
- 8 cups homemade chicken stock (or canned chicken broth)
- 1 (14-ounce) can fire-roasted diced tomatoes (or Ro-tel tomatoes and chiles)
- 1 cup hominy
- 2 (15-ounce) cans black beans, drained and rinsed
- 1 (4-ounce) can diced green chiles
- 2 teaspoons salt
- 4 corn tortillas, cut into strips
- Juice of 2 limes
- Shredded Monterey Jack cheese for serving
- Chopped cilantro for serving

Bring a large pot of water to a boil. Add the chicken breasts and simmer for about 20 minutes, or until cooked through. Drain chicken and set aside to cool. Once cool, chop into 1-inch cubes.

While the chicken is cooking, roast the poblano pepper over a burner on a gas stove or under the broiler until it is very charred (almost black). Set aside on a plate to cool, then dice.

Heat the olive oil in a very large pot over medium-high heat until hot but not smoking, then add the onion and jalapeño and cook, stirring occasionally, until soft, about 5 minutes. Add the garlic and diced poblano and cook for another minute. Add the chili powder and cumin and stir until well combined.

Stir in the chicken stock, diced tomatoes, hominy, black beans, green chiles, diced cooked chicken, and salt and bring to a boil. Add the tortilla strips and lime juice and cook until the tortillas soften.

Serve with the shredded cheese and chopped cilantro on the side.

Homemade Chicken Stock

Makes about 2 quarts

Everyone should have a homemade chicken stock recipe; it really does make a big difference in the flavor of any dish. You can freeze this in small portions for quick and easy defrosting.

1 large chicken, about 5 pounds
1 yellow onion, unpeeled and cut in half
2 large carrots, ends trimmed and cut in half
2 large stalks celery, ends removed, cut in half
1 bay leaf
Cold fresh water

Put chicken in a large stockpot with remaining ingredients. Add cold water to cover. Put pot over high heat and bring to a boil, then reduce heat to a simmer, partially cover, and simmer for two hours. Skim any scum that rises to the top.

After two hours, remove the chicken from the pot and remove the veggies. Then, bring the stock back up to a boil and cook until it has reduced by half. This should take another hour or two.

Cool the stock, then strain through a fine-mesh strainer into a clean stockpot. If desired, freeze individual portions of stock in sandwich-sized plastic bags, then defrost as needed.

9

HOME FOR
THE HOLIDAYS

I HEADED HOME FOR THE HOLIDAYS AFTER MEAT FABRICATION class, exhausted both mentally and physically. Helen was going home as well, and despite our very different career choices, we both felt the exact same way. The other night over sushi she had finally confided in me that she felt she might have made a mistake in joining the police force.

"It's not really what I thought," she had said, as she picked at some lightly salted edamame. We had gone out to dinner to celebrate the end of my first semester and the impending Christmas break. "It's not that I don't think I can do it, but I'm just not all that happy. I keep thinking it will get better, but it's getting worse."

Orlando had a tough crime scene, and Helen looked as if she hadn't slept in weeks. I wasn't sure she had.

As we prepared to go our separate ways for the holiday break, we hugged and promised to stay in touch over the next few weeks. Then she jumped in her SUV and turned toward the interstate. I only had an hour and a half drive home but was looking forward to it. I needed to clear my head a little bit. Though I hadn't told anybody yet, I was also beginning to second-guess my decision to go back to school. I hadn't made many friends and constantly felt alienated because I was the only person there who didn't aspire to be a chef. Now, three months in, I was worried that I had made the wrong decision.

It didn't help matters that people were constantly asking me why I would go to culinary school in the first place if I didn't want to be a restaurant chef. I patiently explained again and again that the art of writing about food required actually *knowing* food. If I didn't really know the subject I was writing about, how could I ever be taken seriously? I had read many writers who could give beautiful, mouth-watering descriptions of food, but their eloquent prose seemed to lack a deeper knowledge. I wanted to be the writer who *really* knew what she was talking about, who understood *why* a given dish worked or didn't work. But I was starting to doubt myself. Was culinary school really the way to achieve my goals?

As I turned the corner onto my parents' street, my anxious thoughts melted away, and I felt relief wash over me.

"Jen's back!" my brother shouted as I opened the door.

"Hey, John, what's goin' on?" I said. My little brother wasn't so little anymore, and he towered over me. I noticed the faint shadow above his lip and the way his arms seemed to fill out his white short-sleeve shirt. He was five years my junior, and through our whole lives we had maintained a very standard "little brother–big sister" relationship. We fought. We yelled. We bickered. But at the end of the day, he was my little brother and I loved him.

"Nothin,'" he said, and threw open the fridge to grab a Coke.

My parents came down the stairs and hugged me. "Welcome home, sweetie," my mom said.

"We were hoping you could debone our chicken for dinner tonight," Dad said, winking.

"Ha, ha. Very funny. I think I'm ready to take a little break from animals." I set my suitcase near the stairs and followed everyone into the kitchen. "How's school going, John?" I asked.

"Fine. Boring." A typical seventeen-year-old's answer. "Hey, Mom? Can I go to David's house now?" he asked.

Mom sighed. "We would love to have you stay for dinner, John, but if you really want to go, you can go."

"Great. See ya, Jen!" John shouted as he slammed the front door behind him.

Mom had made a delicious pasta dish using fettuccine, Brie cheese, and escarole, the slightly bitter green. She served heaping portions to my dad and me, alongside a simple green salad. I loved how the Brie coated every strand of slippery fettuccine and perfectly rounded out the flavor of the spicy greens. Mom was such a fabulous cook, and she took pride in feeding her family well with dishes that were not only tasty but healthy, too.

Later that evening, I lay in my childhood bed and considered my options. I hadn't let on to my parents that anything was wrong; I just needed time to really think. I could keep going, I could drop out, or . . . I could switch to the Pastry and Baking Program, the other culinary option offered at my school. I hadn't given the P&B program much thought when I enrolled. It cost about the same as the Culinary program, and I just figured since I was there, I might as well do the whole shebang.

The next day, I sat in my closet, organizing clothes I never wore anymore and going through old pairs of shoes, deciding what to take

back to Orlando with me and what to donate to Goodwill. I was reach-
ing up to grab a shoebox from the top shelf when a bright orange
plastic box fell down, scattering note cards all over my closet floor.
I jumped down from the chair I had been standing on and picked up
one of the cards. The script was tiny and faded, but I could make out
an old-fashioned recipe for Ritz Pie. I knew immediately that the box
once had belonged to my great-grandmother, but had no idea how it
had found its way into my closet.

"Mom!" I ran into her room with the Ritz Pie recipe in one hand
and the orange box in the other. "Where did this come from?" I asked,
holding out the box for her to see.

"Oh, I had totally forgotten about that! Grandma gave me that to
give to you. Those are all of Great-Grandma's recipes from when she
had the bakery during World War Two. Grandma thought you might
like to have them," my mom said, a smile growing on her face.

I had almost forgotten about my great-grandmother, who had
worked as a baker and cake decorator during the Second World War,
while her young husband fought on the front lines in Europe. After he
was killed in the war, my great-grandmother had three young children
to support, and she continued to work as a baker for the rest of her life.
She had passed away when I was just a baby, so I never really knew her,
but I wore her tiny emerald-studded ring on my right hand.

"I think she would have wanted you to have these, Jennifer. She
had the best dessert recipes!" Mom said.

Back in my room, I carefully went through the cards, sitting cross-
legged with them scattered all around me. I could have sworn they
still smelled of spun sugar and buttercream icing. There were recipes

for Swedish ginger cookies, sour-cream coffee cake, and a very retro chocolate pie made with saltine crackers and whipped cream. Other recipes called for old-fashioned ingredients such as clabbered milk and lard, and I immediately started thinking of how I could remake these desserts in a modern-day kitchen. I was taken with the story, the faded handwriting, and the recipes themselves, and suddenly all I wanted to do was bake. What if I reworked all these recipes for a more modern kitchen and then wrote a book about it? My heart started fluttering. Yes, I thought, that's what I will do. It was perfect! I could combine my passions for food, writing, and history all in one. But first, I would need to know how to rewrite the recipes.

The whole thing seemed like an answered prayer. I no longer stressed about my decision to go to culinary school, and instead prepared to tell my parents about my new decision: to switch over to the Baking and Pastry Program. It was perfect, really. I could swap my hours at the restaurant for a day shift and then go to school at night, when the B&P program took place. I would learn everything possible about baking, and then when I graduated, I would work on Great-Grandma's recipe collection. I couldn't wait.

Come to think of it, I didn't love to carve pork. I didn't even *really* love to chop carrots. What did I love to do more than anything? Bake. It's been said that most people can cook but not everyone can bake, and I had always found solace and comfort in reading recipes and watching bread rise. I loved the fact that if you followed the recipe's instructions, the final product would turn out as expected. In a world with no real guarantees, the fact that I was promised sugar cookies in one hour if I read the fine print in my big yellow *Gourmet* bible was an unmitigated joy. I was sure that switching to the B&P program was the answer to my prayers and, that night, I prepared to tell my parents the news over dinner.

My mom was serving up slices of perfectly cooked roast pork when I piped up.

"I have an announcement to make!" I said. "I've decided that I want to switch over from the Culinary Program to the Baking and Pastry Program at school."

Mom and Dad raised their eyebrows while John stuffed a large piece of pork in his mouth. "Honey?" Dad said. "What brought this on? I thought things were going well at school."

I sighed. "It's been . . . fine. I just haven't been one hundred percent happy, and with the kind of money I'm spending to go, I want to actually enjoy my time there."

I chewed on a piece of pork and instantly memories of Meat Fab came flooding back, leaving an almost bitter taste in my mouth. I had been so looking forward to my mom's cooking during this break, but this was not what I'd expected. After dealing solely with chopping up animals for the past month, I had simply lost my appetite for meat. I couldn't help but notice, though, the color of the pork and wonder if it had been cooked to a proper 160 degrees. I just couldn't seem to escape meat, no matter where I was.

"But are you sure you want to do this?" Mom asked, a look of worry in her eyes. "I thought you said getting a general degree in culinary arts was looked at with higher regard in the actual job market . . . . You don't want to transfer now just because it's easier and then have a harder time later getting a job!"

"Mom, you know I don't want to be a restaurant chef anyway!" I said. "My passion isn't for cooking chicken, it's for baking. Finding Great-Grandma's recipe box solidified that. I want to learn everything possible about baking and desserts so that I know enough to rewrite her recipes." I didn't add that I had already found out that some of my credits would transfer over, so I'd still be able to graduate at the same time. I gingerly sliced through my pork again, seeing visions of the whole animals that I had just broken down a few days before.

"Well, you're right. It is your money and your time. If you think switching programs is best, we trust you," Dad said with a smile.

Later, my mom came up to my room and lightly knocked on the door. I was sitting in my pajamas on my bed, with Great-Grandma's recipes spread out all over my comforter.

"Jenny Ren?" Mom called softly. "Can I come in?"

Jenny Ren was her pet name for me, a name she had been calling me since I was a baby, even though no one else in the world did.

"Of course, come on in!" I called.

Mom was wearing her pajamas, too, and her shoulder-length blonde hair was pulled up in a ponytail. Growing up, I always wanted to be just like her, and it sometimes struck me how similar we'd become as I'd grown older.

"I just wanted you to know that I'm proud of you . . . really. Great-Grandma would be proud of you, too. I think you're making the right decision," she said, sitting down on the edge of my bed and picking up one of the faded recipe cards.

I smiled. "Thanks," I said.

"You always did have that stubborn streak in you, just like Grandpa. Once you get your mind wrapped around something, there's no turning back, is there?" Mom let out a soft laugh and reached over to gently squeeze my shoulder. "But I think baking is much more up your alley," she added.

I could hear John's video games almost shaking the bedroom wall, and Mom rolled her eyes. "See, or rather *hear*, what you're missing? That boy will be the death of me."

I thought about asking my brother to go to a movie over the break, but I knew he would say no. We had never been very close, but I had always wanted and wished for a best-friend type of sibling relationship. With my living away from home and his being a sullen teenager, that seemed almost impossible now. Still, it couldn't hurt to try. I just hoped he wasn't falling in with the wrong crowd at school. Mom reassured me he wasn't, but I had my doubts. A few times I thought I had smelled pot in his car, but when I tried to confront him about it he just laughed it off and denied anything. John had been pushing the limits in every way since we were kids; he was as much of a rebel as I was a conservative rule-follower, and I hoped he was staying safe. Mom had also casually mentioned that a few times a very cute, soft-spoken girl with long brown hair had been hanging around the house. Of course, whenever she brought it up with John, he turned bright red, muttered a one-word response, and ran up the stairs.

I laughed and chatted with Mom for a while longer before turning off the light and climbing into bed. A sense of peace washed over me that I hadn't felt in quite a while. I still had almost two whole weeks at home to think and plan for the change. There would be no more butchery, no more precision cuts, and no more bleeding all over the onions.

Linguine with Escarole and Brie

Serves 4

Peppery escarole, creamy Brie cheese, and salty, crisp bacon—in a word, delicious!
If you can't find escarole, use kale instead.

8 ounces dry linguine pasta
2 ounces bacon, chopped
1 large garlic clove, minced
1 shallot, minced
1 pound fresh escarole, chopped into 1-inch ribbons
½ pound Brie cheese, rind removed and cheese diced into
      medium-size cubes (it doesn't matter if the cubes
      aren't perfect!)
Salt and freshly ground black pepper to taste

Cook the pasta according to package directions in a pot of boiling salt water until *al dente*.

Meanwhile, cook the bacon in a large skillet until crispy. Add the garlic and shallot and cook for another two minutes, stirring well. Add the escarole and toss together, cooking until wilted.

When the pasta is cooked, drain it (reserving ½ cup cooking water). Toss the pasta with the escarole in the skillet until well combined, then add the Brie. Cook until the Brie begins to melt, adding a little of the extra cooking water if the pasta gets too dry.

Season with salt and pepper and serve.

Old-Fashioned Chocolate-Walnut Torte

Serves 6

Ahh, the dessert of my childhood. This torte screams "retro," and you'll never guess the secret ingredient.

2 egg whites
1¼ cups granulated sugar, divided
20 saltines, crushed
2 cups heavy cream
3 tablespoons cocoa powder, plus additional for dusting
1½ cups chopped walnuts

Preheat the oven to 325°F. Heavily grease two cake pans with butter (cooking spray won't work here).

Beat the egg whites with an electric mixer on high speed. When you can't see the bottom of the bowl, slowly add 1 cup of the granulated sugar, continuing to beat on high, until stiff, glossy peaks form. Fold saltines into meringue.

Spread meringue over the bottoms of cake pans and bake for 25 minutes. Transfer the meringues in the pans to a wire rack to cool completely.

Meanwhile, whip the cream with the cocoa powder and the remaining ¼ cup sugar. Fold in walnuts.

When meringues are cool, gently peel them out of the cake pans. This might be difficult, but it's easiest if you run a knife very gently underneath the meringue to loosen it up a bit. Don't worry if it breaks a little—you'll be covering the whole thing in whipped cream anyway, so no one will know the difference.

Spread half of the whipped cream onto one meringue layer. Gently place the other layer on top and top with remaining whipped cream. Spread meringue evenly over the sides of the meringues, then dust top with cocoa powder.

10
MOVING ON

PULLED INTO MY APARTMENT PARKING SPOT, TRUNK FILLED WITH suitcases and groceries, eager to see Helen again after two weeks apart. She had gotten home a few hours before I did, and we were planning on cooking something easy for dinner together that night. My arms were full as I flung open the door and shouted inside, "Mella!" using my childhood name for her. When we were seven, Helen's grandmother from Greece taught us our Greek names—mine was Yonulla— and we had been using them for each other ever since. It started as a childhood joke, but somehow it still stuck almost fifteen years later.

Helen walked into the kitchen wearing dark jeans and a black shirt, with her hair done up in a messy knot on the top of her head. Without ever seeming to try, she always managed to look fashionable.

She gave me a big hug. "Yonulla! I've missed you!" she said.

"I missed you, too. I can't wait to be filled in on everything over dinner. Want to go out?" I asked while starting to unload the groceries.

"Sounds perfect. I've been craving some good Pad Thai lately. Do you need help bringing in anything from downstairs?" she asked, and I couldn't help but notice how much healthier and more rested she looked than when we'd parted only two weeks ago. The dark circles had pretty much faded entirely from around her eyes, and she seemed relaxed and full of life.

"Nope, I got them all. Thanks, though. I'm just going to unpack a little, then I'll freshen up and be ready for dinner," I said.

I couldn't wait to tell Helen the news of my decision to switch programs. I had one more general culinary class to get through before I could officially make the switch, but that class happened to be Introduction to Baking, so I was excited regardless. Tomorrow I would have to talk to the registrar's office, and I also needed to talk to Tony at work to make sure I could swap my night shift for daytime. Everything seemed to be falling perfectly into place, and I couldn't wait to get going.

We got to the restaurant around six and headed to our favorite booth in the back. It seemed like just yesterday we were here after moving into the apartment, before this new phase in our lives ever really started. Right after our Pad Thai came, as I was swirling my first long noodle around my fork, Helen cleared her throat.

"So . . . I made some decisions over break," she began, looking down at her plate. Whatever she was about to say was clearly well thought out but difficult. "After talking with my mom and dad, I've decided to quit the police force and move back to Naples for a while, while I figure out what I really want to do." Helen bit her lip. "I'm really sorry, Jenna. I wish there were an easier solution."

I sat stunned. What about our apartment? What about being roommates, just like we talked about when we were eight years old? This was supposed to be our fun year together, and now Helen was moving away. I could never afford our place on my own and had never lived by myself before. I was both mad and sad at the same time. I remembered the time in fifth grade when my family moved away and I was sent to a new junior high all by myself. Helen and I had had a sleepover on our last night in my house, and we stayed up late telling secrets and promising each other that nothing was really going change. The next day, though, as my parents' minivan pulled away, leaving Helen and her mom in our old driveway, fat tears rolled down my cheeks. I had never felt so alone. My new school was cold and unfriendly; all of the other kids in my grade already had set groups of friends and teased me about my glasses and my skinny, undeveloped body. Once the boys found out that I didn't wear a bra, I got taunted endlessly and ended up hiding in the shower stall during P.E., writing tear-stained letters to Helen.

"Oh," I said. "But why are you moving home? Couldn't you figure things out here?" I asked her.

Helen looked sad. "I think I already have a temporary job lined up at home until I make more decisions. It just makes more sense for me to move back in with my parents right now because they're willing to help me a little bit. Nothing is set in stone though . . . I just really wasn't happy doing what I was doing. But don't worry, I'm still going to pay half the rent from home. I don't want you feeling stuck now that I'm leaving."

"When are you going?" I asked her. My first day back at school was the next day, and every night that week I was scheduled at the restaurant. The calm of Christmas break was about to be broken.

"In a few days. I'm packing up now," she said.

"Well then! I guess that pretty much covers everything," I said tartly and then concentrated on my dinner. I hated myself for responding like that, but the words had just flown out of my mouth.

Helen made a sad face. "Don't be mad at me, Yonulla. I just had to do something because I was getting depressed. This isn't going to change anything, really."

I knew it would, though. I had just found my best friend again after years apart, only to lose her once more. She would move home, I would continue with school, and we would both move on.

I sighed. "I'm not mad at you, I'm just bummed. I don't want you depressed or unhappy, so this is obviously the best choice. I'll just miss you, that's all."

We changed the subject to lighter things, chatting about Rob and Michael and our brothers. She asked me how John was doing and I rolled my eyes.

"He's such a teenager," I said. "Only thinks about himself and just wants to have fun. I'm kind of worried he might be hanging out with a bad crowd." I didn't mention that Mom had found a pack of cigarettes in his trunk last week.

"I'm sure he's fine. Teenage guys all go through that stage."

"Yeah . . . I just want to make sure he's okay, you know? It seems like just yesterday he was five and we were pushing him around in that wheelbarrow."

Helen laughed hysterically. "Oh my gosh, I'll never forget that. Remember how you used to dress him up like a pioneer and tell him we were going on the Oregon Trail?"

"Ha! Those were the days. We were so weird," I said, laughing now, too. Back then, everything seemed so uncomplicated.

When we got home, I ironed my chef's uniform and laid out everything for the morning. I couldn't wait to make my switch official and dive deep into the world of bread, cookies, and pastries.

The next morning, I gathered all my tools and headed to school earlier than usual. At 6:45 a.m., the hallways were still quiet, but the aromas of freshly roasted coffee and scrambled eggs wafted in from the cafeteria. I made my way to the classroom kitchen where Introduction to Baking I was being held. There were only two other students in the kitchen so far, and I recognized one of the guys from Basic Skills setting up his station. This classroom kitchen was different from any other I had been in so far, with long wooden (not metal) tables down the center and industrial-size ovens all along the wall. In the back of the kitchen, the biggest stand mixers I had ever seen were propped up against the wall, ready to cream butter and sugar into thick ribbons. The kitchen smelled slightly of yeast, but the best thing about it was that it was *warm*. Gone were the days of wearing little boys' long underwear underneath my chef's whites and gripping hot tea to keep from shivering.

A very small woman wearing glasses and a large chef's hat was at the front of the room, weighing flour on an old-fashioned kitchen scale. I set my pastry tool kit down on an end of one of the long tables and made my way to the front to introduce myself.

"Hi, Chef, I'm Jenna," I said.

Chef looked up at me over the tops of her glasses and smiled warmly. "Hi, Jenna! I'm Chef Tolby. It's nice to meet you."

Finally, a chef who didn't appear to be hostile or a member of the Green Berets. Chef Tolby was a sweet older woman who later told us that she had worked as the head pastry chef at a number of Europe's best restaurants before moving back to the United States and "retiring" to teach. She stood only a little over five feet tall but was bursting with enthusiasm and passion for baking. I could already tell I would learn a lot from her. When I told her that I was making the switch to the Baking and Pastry program, she smiled wide, eyes crinkling, and welcomed me. For the first time yet, we weren't assigned partners or groups in class. Chef Tolby said that it was important for all of us to learn basic baking principles on our own, without the constant aid of teammates. I've always worked better solo, and I liked this plan a lot. As in my two previous classes, though, we would have practicals every Friday morning that were worth a large percentage of our grade. As Chef Tolby went over the syllabus, I paged through the notebook she had just handed out. On the list of things to make were chocolate-chip cookies, croissants, sponge cake, and pizza dough. Finally, I felt right at home.

After Chef finished her short lecture, we were set loose to work on our first recipe: biscuits. I turned the page in my notebook and smoothed down the recipe. Then, I cleared my area and dug for my measuring spoons in my tool kit. Though we were given small electronic scales as part of our initial culinary kit, Chef Tolby wanted us to become familiar with the old, weighted kitchen scales first because, she explained, "you never know what your future restaurant will have." There was already a line forming around the enormous flour bins at the back of the room, and I grabbed my bowl and made my way there. We needed equal parts all-purpose flour and pastry flour, along with sugar and vegetable shortening. I loved not having to rely on anyone else to get the work done, and as soon as all my ingredients were properly weighed and measured, I let myself drift in my baking zone, where all I had to worry about was following the recipe and everything else would just fall into place.

Forty minutes later, the scent of freshly baked biscuits permeated the kitchen. Chef Tolby made rounds, stopping at each of our stations and asking how it was going. My biscuits had turned out perfectly—light, airy, and huge with golden-brown bottoms and lightly toasted tops. I let them cool while cleaning my station and sweeping the floor, then brought them up to Chef to be graded at the end of class.

"Beautiful, Miss Weber! I think you might have found your calling," Chef said as she picked up one of my biscuits and broke it in half to inspect the inner crumb.

I blushed, feeling my confidence rise a few notches. It was exactly the boost I needed after last month's Meat Fabrication debacle. "Thank you, Chef. I really loved baking these."

"I can tell. They look wonderful."

I took my tray back to my station and prepared to do the thing I had been looking forward to for the past five hours: I broke open a biscuit and brought half to my lips. It tasted like butter and toast, and the crumbs melted quickly on the tip of my tongue. Eating it reminded me of the weekly "breakfast for dinner" night at my sorority house during my one semester at University of Alabama. Piles of fluffy buttermilk biscuits were split open and stuffed with scrambled eggs and bacon, and it was always my favorite meal of the week. Missy, our sorority house cook, made amazing biscuits—but this one that now lay half eaten on my cutting board definitely tasted just as good, if not better. I discreetly wrapped the other half in a paper towel and stuffed it in my tool kit for later.

When I got home from class that day, I remembered the biscuit half. I scooped it out and quickly reheated it in the microwave before layering on a piece of ham and some cheddar cheese for a quick prework snack. Helen was busy packing up her room into the same cardboard boxes that she had unpacked only a few months before. I shouted hello with my mouth full and then made my way into my bedroom, leaving a trail of crumbs behind me.

First-Day-of-Class Biscuits

Makes one dozen biscuits

This recipe guarantees fluffy biscuits every time, unless you forget the baking powder. Serve them split open with butter and your favorite jam.

> 2 cups pastry flour
> 2 cups all-purpose flour
> 2 tablespoons granulated sugar
> 1 teaspoon salt
> 2 teaspoons baking powder
> ½ teaspoon baking soda
> ½ cup shortening, chilled and cut into small pieces
> ¾ cup buttermilk

Preheat the oven to 400°F. Line a baking sheet with parchment paper and set aside.

In a large bowl, mix together pastry flour, all-purpose flour, sugar, salt, baking powder, and baking soda. Add shortening and mix well with your hands until the mixture resembles tiny grains of sand.

Form a well in the center of the dough and pour in the buttermilk. Mix only until combined. Turn dough out onto a floured surface and knead five times. With a rolling pin, roll out dough ½-inch thick.

Cut biscuits using biscuit cutters or the rim of a large glass. Place biscuits on lined baking sheet and bake until golden, 12 to 15 minutes.

Serve with honey butter, raspberry jam, or ham and cheese.

Spicy Sesame Noodle Bowls

Serves 4

Whenever I have a craving for Vietnamese food, I head to the kitchen and make this recipe. Cooked shrimp make a nice addition.

1 cup soy sauce
1 cup hot water
1 cup canola oil
1 cup tahini (sesame seed paste)
⅓ cup sugar
½ cup cider vinegar
¼ cup chili oil
2½ tablespoons toasted sesame oil
5 cloves garlic, minced
8 ounces soba noodles, cooked, drained, and rinsed with cold
    water (drizzle with sesame oil after cooking)
Sesame seeds for garnish
Sliced raw veggies of your choice (red pepper strips, carrot sticks,
    bean sprouts)

In a large bowl, mix together the soy sauce and hot water until combined and smooth. Add canola oil and mix again, then add tahini, sugar, and vinegar, mixing well after each addition. Add chili oil, sesame oil, and garlic. Whisk until everything is combined.

Serve with cold-cooked noodles and top with sesame seeds and raw vegetables.

11

BREAKING BREAD

FINALLY, IT WAS THE FIRST NIGHT OF MY FIRST OFFICIAL BAKING and Pastry class. I had switched over to the program effortlessly, a matter of a few signed papers and swapping my old knives and culinary tools for more baker-friendly gear. I now had more measuring cups and spoons, a wooden rolling pin, and a brand-new set of pastry tips that I couldn't wait to test out.

Helen had moved home a week earlier. Before she left, she'd promised again to continue paying her share of the monthly rent. We gave each other a big hug. When her SUV pulled out of the drive, I went back inside the apartment and stood in the silence. Then, I made myself a fancy dinner and went to bed early. Part of me thought I would actually enjoy living by myself. I was so busy, anyway, and hardly ever there to begin with. I could leave dirty dishes in the sink, go to bed early without an excuse, and blast my music while getting dressed for work in the morning. It was freeing.

And now here I was. With my whites on, my flour out, ready to roll on the first night of class. Bread 101, it was called. I had already read the first chapters in the textbook and couldn't wait to get started. During this class, we would be learning all about bread, starting with the basics of bread science like flour type and gluten, and then moving on to baking classic French and American breads.

My instructor, Chef Hill, had quite a reputation with the ladies as being the most attractive chef in school. He had shoulder-length wavy brown hair, deep blue eyes, and a permanent five o'clock shadow on his face. He'd worked as an artisanal baker for years and had the well-muscled arms and hands of someone who kneaded bread all day long.

During lineup, he looked me up and down and wrote a few notes in his planner. "Thanks, that'll do," he said, and snapped his book shut. I was the last person in line and hustled back to my seat at the front of the kitchen. I eagerly absorbed everything he said about different types of flour, gluten, wild yeast, and oven temperatures. I loved the warmth of the oven, the feel of the flour on my fingertips, and even the scent of the pungent fresh yeast, which felt like velvet but crumbled in the palm of my hand. My first bread from scratch was a loaf of traditional French bread, with a hard, crusty exterior and a soft, chewy center. By the third day, I couldn't tell if I was more in love with the way Chef Hill looked as he plunged his tanned hands into a big pile of dough, or the way baking homemade bread made me feel— alive and talented. I loved learning and taking notes about different countries' bread-making traditions, and there was nothing quite like eating homemade bread straight out of the oven, either.

In that class, I made my first real culinary-school friend. Her name was Samantha and she lived in Melbourne, Florida, about an hour's drive south, right next to my hometown of Vero Beach. We had moved to Vero Beach when I was eleven, and only recently had my parents decided to make the move across the state to Tampa. To me, Vero would always feel like home.

Samantha was of medium height and had gorgeous mahogany-colored hair, which she said she'd dyed pink and blue at one point in her life. She had a unique obsession with Disney World and had even gone so far as to get married at Epcot Center a few years earlier. We'd set up our stations next to each other on the first night of Breads and had been chatting away ever since. Samantha wanted to become a cake decorator after she graduated, and from the sketches she had shown me, the girl had talent.

The two of us also befriended a guy around our age named Jake. He was serious and intelligent, having just graduated from a small honors college in Florida the year before. He was the first student I'd met who had actually obtained a bachelor's degree before entering culinary school, and over nightly cleanups we would talk about our favorite books and college classes. Jake was just as serious about baking bread as I was, if not more so, and he wanted to open an artisanal bakery when he graduated. On the fourth night of class, Chef Hill paired the two of us as partners for the duration of the class, and I was relieved to finally have found a partner with whom I really clicked.

Breads 101 is also where we finally made the food that had featured so prominently in my culinary-school fantasies: croissants. Jake and I took turns rolling whole sticks of butter into the soft dough, then folding it back up into a tight square and rolling it out again, until all of the butter had been incorporated and the dough was smooth.

"This is fun, isn't it?" Jake asked as I folded the big blob of dough and stacked it on top of itself.

"I love this," I said. "I finally feel like I've found some sort of calling, and it comes so naturally. There are no pots on the stove, no onions to be chopped or hot grease splattering. It's just us and the dough."

Samantha, who was working nearby with her partner, another wannabe wedding-cake decorator, chimed in. "I agree! And who wouldn't want to work with Chef Hill?"

Jake rolled his eyes, and I laughed as I carried our dough away to place in the proofing box to rise. Later, we would punch it down and then roll it out super thin before carefully cutting it into triangles and shaping them into croissants. I mixed an egg wash to brush over the tops of the unbaked croissants. Jake was busy scraping bits of dried dough off the work surface.

Twenty minutes later, we had a dozen flimsy triangles on the floured counter in front of us. I opened my textbook to the diagrams depicting how to fold the croissants and got started. The dough felt soft and sticky under my fingertips. I had just finished rolling up my first one and placing it on the parchment-lined sheet pan in front of me when Chef Hill strolled by.

"How are you doing there, Weber?" he asked.

"Fine, Chef. Should the dough be this soft, though?" I held up a sticky triangle for him to see.

"Yep, that's perfect. Just be sure to keep enough flour on your table so the dough doesn't stick. And roll up tight, but not too tight." He started rolling one of my triangles to demonstrate. "It looks like you guys are on the right track. Good work."

Chef then turned to the class and announced in a loud voice, "Guys, I forgot to tell you, but there's a box of chocolate over in the back that you can use if you want to make a few *pains au chocolat*."

I looked at Jake and he nodded with a grin.

"Hey, grab me a few, too," Samantha called as I made my way to the back of the kitchen. Chocolate croissants always made me think of the summer I spent studying abroad in Paris. Late in the day, between classes, I would go into a local bakery and get a flaky, sweet *pain au chocolat* as an afternoon snack. I would take my prize to the Luxembourg Gardens and sit in the grass and people-watch, the chocolate smearing on my fingers and little bits of flaky pastry fluttering around me. I grabbed a big handful of the dark chocolate tablets from the box and brought them back to our table.

"Sweet!" Jake said as he took a piece of chocolate and set it in the center of his dough triangle.

I nibbled on two pieces of the chocolate before stuffing my croissants. Then I brushed all of our pastries with egg wash and carried them to the oven to bake. They came out golden brown and puffy, and a few had chocolate oozing out the sides. I bit into the runt of the batch immediately. Instantly, the crumbs melted on my tongue and I was left with chocolate-covered fingers and a very big smile. Gone were all the initial hesitations about culinary school; this was one hundred percent where I belonged.

By the second week, I felt more than ready for our first practical on French bread. It was Friday night, and I had on a clean, spotless chef jacket and starched white apron. I had studied for hours the day before, so I felt pretty confident that I knew the baking procedure and correct temperatures. For the practical, we were not allowed to use our textbooks but could refer to the notes we had taken in class. Chef Hill sat up at the front of the kitchen and gave us basic instructions and end times, and then we were cut loose. For the first time yet, the kitchen was absolutely silent as students scooped flour into their bowls and weighed out their ingredients. Jake and Samantha were working next to me, as usual, but we were forbidden to talk at all during the practical. Samantha had dyed a single lock of her hair bright red, and it peeked out of her hairnet.

I gave a nervous smile to my friends and started working on gathering and measuring my ingredients. I took great care in taking the temperature of my water three times to make sure it was a perfect one hundred degrees. I laid out my *mise en place* bowls, sifted my flour, and checked the weights on my scale meticulously. Pretty soon, I had a large, sticky ball of dough in my hands, which I covered with plastic wrap and set on the table to rest for an hour. Then, I scrubbed bits of crusted flour out from underneath my fingernails and cleaned up my area so that everything was organized and ready for the next step. After the dough had risen, I punched it down, expelling any gas, and worked with lightly floured hands to make one long *batard*, or roughly football-shaped loaf. The most difficult part of this process was making sure all the seams were pinched tightly on the bottom so that the loaf didn't unroll or explode in the oven, which had happened when a few students took this practical earlier in the week. Using a paring knife, I gently scored three parallel, diagonal slashes down the length of the dough to allow steam to escape from the bread while it baked. Finally, I dusted a sheet pan with cornmeal, laid my sticky *batard* on top, and carried the tray to the proof box to rise for another hour.

When my timer went off, I anxiously opened the door of the proof box. But instead of the large, puffy mound of dough that I expected to find, my dough resembled a beat-up old couch, deflated and lumpy. I gasped out loud. *What went wrong? What did I do?* I had weighed out my ingredients perfectly and had checked my scale numerous times for accuracy. My water temperature had been exactly one hundred degrees, and I had made sure to grab the new, fresh yeast from the cooler. I had done everything right. This wasn't supposed to happen, especially on the night of a practical! I carried the lump of dough back to my station and wordlessly plopped it down on the floured tabletop. Unable to give any guidance, Jake just looked at it with an expression of shock. I sighed and shrugged my shoulders, feeling like I might cry but not wanting to embarrass myself. Instead, I considered my options. I could show it to Chef now and be done with it, or I could start over. One quick glance at the clock told me I didn't have enough time to start over; finished products were due in to Chef in an hour. I looked back and forth from my dead dough to Chef Hill's gorgeous blue eyes and felt overcome with nausea. I had no choice but to swallow my pride and bake my flat loaf, hoping that five hundred degrees and steam could work some kind of miracle.

As I loaded the blob of dough into the oven, other students gave me sympathetic looks. We all knew that practicals were a huge chunk of our grade. Twenty minutes later, not much had changed—my *batard* was nothing but a very ugly, flat piece of bread, a bit burned around the edges and certainly not hollow inside like it should have been. I carried it up to the front.

"Weber, this yours?" Chef Hill waved his hand at my monstrosity.

I felt pinpricks in the back of my throat and anxiously wiped my palms on my checkered pants. "Yes, Chef," I said.

Chef made a clicking sound and thumped the bottom of the loaf with his fingers.

"I'm just not quite sure what happened. . . . I scaled everything right; I know I did!" I was trying not to cry as the rest of the class circled around to see an example of what French bread should *not* look like.

Chef looked up. "It's dead, Weber. Dead yeast. Your yeast must have gotten in contact with the salt and that killed it. Remember my lecturing about that on the first night of class? I said be careful, under *no circumstances* should your yeast touch your salt!"

"Yeah, that's right," I mumbled. "I don't know how it happened."

"It's fine, Weber. Happens to the best of us. Now, taste it." He broke off a tough piece and pointed it at me.

I looked up at him in horror with no other option than to accept the flat bread and put it in my mouth. Immediately, my mouth began to salivate as all I could taste was pure salt. It tasted like a salt lick, the kind you'd give to a horse, but worse. I chewed and swallowed. My tongue was raw, and the bite of bread sat in my stomach like the rock it was.

"That'll teach you a lesson, Miss Weber. Never, *ever* let your salt touch your yeast," Chef Hill said before jotting down a large, red *C* in his grade book.

Whole-Wheat Pizza Dough

Makes enough dough for two medium (10-inch) pizzas

This never-fail pizza dough produces the most amazingly chewy crust. Since the recipe makes enough dough for two pies, you can either have a party or freeze half in a plastic bag for the next time.

1 packet (¼ oz) dry yeast
1⅓ cups warm water
2 cups all-purpose flour
1½ cups whole-wheat flour
1½ teaspoons sea salt
1 tablespoon olive oil, plus additional for rubbing dough

In the bowl of a stand mixer, combine yeast and warm water and let mixture sit for 5 minutes for the yeast to dissolve completely.

In a small bowl, mix together flours and salt. Turn stand mixer to medium-high speed and add flour mixture slowly to yeast.* Drizzle in olive oil. Mix for 5 minutes, until the dough is soft and elastic.

Remove dough from mixer bowl, rub dough with more olive oil, and return it to the bowl. Cover with a dish towel and place in a warm spot to rise for one hour.

After dough has doubled in size, cut it in half to make dough for two large pizzas. I like to freeze one large ball of dough for a later use.

When you are ready to make your pizza, roll out the dough, cover with toppings of your choice, and bake at 425°F for 10–15 minutes.

* The salt in the yeast is fine here because the yeast you are using isn't fresh and the salt isn't coming into direct contact with it.

NOTE: My favorite pizza toppings are simply fresh goat cheese, sliced tomatoes, and mushrooms. Cover your pizza with the cheese of your choice and the toppings you like best. You could also add a pinch of red pepper flakes for a spicy kick. In my opinion, the more goat cheese the better.

12
WRITTEN IN CHOCOLATE

IT WAS SEVEN O'CLOCK ON MONDAY MORNING, AND I WAS hunched over my kitchen table gripping a parchment pastry bag with both hands, trying desperately to keep myself steady as I drizzled chocolate cursive letters on wax paper. A steaming cup of Earl Grey tea sat next to me, along with a now-empty bowl of oatmeal. I had chocolate smeared on my forearm and below one eye, the result of having attempted to push a strand of hair behind my ear a moment before. I'd awakened early that morning to practice my chocolate writing, since I would be at work all day and needed to get this down before class tonight.

I also enjoyed working early in the morning, when everything was calm and quiet. My favorite time to read, write, and cook was just as the sun was coming up, and I always felt that if I worked hard in the morning, I could relax at night. Now, however, that wasn't the case, since I usually didn't get out of school until midnight most nights. Classes were supposed to end at 11:30, but we rarely ended on time; there was always that last dish to be washed or bag of garbage to be taken out.

I had spent the previous weekend at home with Rob and my parents. I had a wonderful time, but I felt a strange sense of relief upon returning to my empty apartment, school, and work. On Saturday night, Rob and I had gone to a friend's engagement party, which ended with the same tension that had recently been plaguing our relationship. All of Rob's friends were older than I was and in very different life stages. They were all great people, and I knew it was important to Rob for me to be friends with his friends' wives, but I never felt like I quite fit in with them. I was the quiet one, the conservative one who would rather stay home and read a book than go out and get drunk at a bar downtown. For the most part, Rob respected my introverted ways, but he still didn't believe I was trying my best to connect with his friends. *If he only knew*, I thought. On Saturday night, I had overheard three of his friends' wives drunkenly discussing how uptight I was and how I never "let loose." My face grew bright red and I felt like I wanted to cry, but all I could do was stay where I was and listen to them size me up. Afterward, not wanting a confrontation, I quickly walked past them as if I hadn't heard a word and found Rob, who was laughing and drinking with a few of his friends from college. We left soon after, and I never told him what I had heard.

My brother was another growing source of stress for me and my family. He had just turned eighteen and seemed to consider himself invincible. The day before I headed back to Orlando, Mom pulled me aside and told me in a worried tone that she had found a few beer bottles hidden in his car. I had feared that he was getting into trouble, and this helped confirm my suspicions, but I knew that my talking to him wouldn't solve anything. To him, I was just the overly anxious big sister. Still, I couldn't help wondering if there was something I could do to help him get back on the right path.

Now, as I sat sipping my tea and practicing my chocolate writing, I let all of that go and just tried to focus at the task at hand. In that moment, I felt confident that John would turn out fine and that Rob would accept the fact that I sometimes would rather spend time alone than with him and his friends. I glanced back up at the clock and saw that it was already almost 8:00 a.m. I squeezed the rest of the still-warm chocolate into a little bowl and balled up my wax paper to throw away. I didn't enjoy my new class, Introduction to Pastries, as much as I had liked Bread 101; the pastry class required a sense of patience and decorating talent that I seemed to lack, no matter how hard I tried. I was much better at the messy jobs, the sticky dough and puffy crois-sants, than I was at rolling fondant, a puttylike icing used to decorate elaborate cakes and *petits fours*, but I was trying.

That night in school, we were making Opera Tortes, a very tradi-tional French *petit four* made up of thin layers of delicate almond sponge cake that had been soaked in coffee liqueur, sandwiched together with coffee buttercream, and topped with a shiny chocolate glaze. The end result was ridiculously rich and delicious, but it took a steady hand to cut the sponge cake evenly. An uneven cut would result in a lopsided torte, which was unacceptable to Chef.

I brought a small stand mixer over to my station and cracked three eggs into the mixing bowl to start the French buttercream, which is essentially beaten eggs mixed with boiling sugar syrup and butter. (Personally, I prefer Italian buttercream, which uses only the egg whites, creating a lighter, airier frosting.) Once my eggs were thick, pale, and ribbonlike, I slowly streamed in my boiling syrup. Pouring too quickly would scramble the eggs, an issue I had already dealt with on my first attempt at making this frosting at home. When all the syrup was added, I cranked the mixer on high and let it go for a good eight minutes while I prepared the rest of my ingredients: two pounds of soft butter, and pure coffee extract, which smelled nothing like Starbucks. My favorite part of making both French and Italian buttercream was the moment after I'd added the butter, soft chunk by soft chunk, when the frosting looked like it was ruined, with tiny chunks of butter floating in a creamy sea. But then, almost like magic, it would come back together and billow up high around the sides of the bowl. It seemed like a good metaphor for life: just when you think that it couldn't get any worse, suddenly things start to look up.

I added two teaspoons of the dark, strong coffee extract to my frosting and stirred. I wondered what all my friends from college were doing right now, on a late Monday night in March. After we'd all graduated, a few friends had gone straight into graduate schools at prestigious Southern universities like Johns Hopkins, UNC Chapel Hill, or University of Virginia. I had lost touch with most of them, since my schedule was not really conducive to spending hours on Facebook or Google Chat. Still, I wouldn't trade staying up late to make frosting for anything, even if it meant losing touch with a few friends.

I felt my cell phone vibrate in my pocket, signaling it was time to check on my almond sponge cakes in the oven. I slid out my sheet tray and peeked in the middle. My cake was perfectly golden and pulling away from the edges of the pan. I breathed a sigh of relief. It wasn't a practical night, but we were preparing pastries for the school's open house tomorrow, when all the parents from the area would come in and see firsthand what their children were up to. We worked in groups again, and I was teamed up with a pair of Spanish-speaking twin sisters two years younger than I was. Most of the time I had no idea what they were saying, but they were hard workers and concerned with their grades. Both Jake and Samantha were in my class, too, but were assigned different groups on the opposite end of the kitchen.

Working carefully, I inverted my sheet cake, then slowly peeled back the parchment paper on top. By itself, the cake was pretty bland. It was a simple sponge cake, using egg whites and powdered almonds folded into a mixture of sugar, butter, and cake flour. The recipe intentionally produced a bland, dry cake because it was meant to be soaked in liqueur, coffee buttercream, and chocolate. A moist, dense cake would crumble under the weight of it all, but a dry cake would be able to absorb everything nicely. I trimmed the edges of my cake and then brushed the liqueur all over the top, followed by a nice big plop of buttercream. Desserts like this seemed so old-fashioned to me, but there really was a special joy in creating them. I felt like anyone could bake muffins or chocolate cupcakes, but assembling a classic Opera Torte really took skill.

As I spread the buttercream across the whole cake with my offset spatula, I thought back upon all the bustling pastry shops on the Left Bank in Paris. Desserts like this one lined the glass cases, and fresh artisanal bread was stacked high on shelves above. Sometimes after school, I would stop in one of the shops on my way home and get a special treat to take home for dessert. Unlike many American women, the French women I met were not concerned with who was the thinnest and who exercised the most. Instead, French women seemed to take much more joy in living a pleasurable life, whether that meant picking up an occasional pastry from the *pâtisserie* or catching up with an old friend for hours over creamy cappuccinos. I missed the Parisian mindset relating to food and life and hoped that after I graduated, I would be able to share it with others.

Later that evening, as my chocolate glaze set up shiny over my torte, I listened to Chef Becker lecture about the next day's events. My dad was coming up for the open house, and I couldn't wait to show off everything I had been working on. The Opera Torte was finished and looking wonderful (only a tiny bit slanted), and my group mates were about to get busy working on the traditional almond *petits fours* and tiny French *macarons*, my favorite. To me, there was not a more perfect cookie than the French *macaron*. Unlike the cloyingly sweet American macaroon, laden with sugary flaked coconut and chocolate, French *macarons* consist of two light almond meringue cookies sandwiched together with a dab of chocolate *ganache* or fruit preserves. I fell in love with these little treats while living in Paris, where they were typically served five to a plate alongside an espresso.

The next day, when my dad arrived, everything was set out perfectly. I had dark circles underneath my eyes from working late the night before, but it was well worth the effort. Our station looked like a mini *pâtisserie*, with all of our pastries arranged over a decorative mirror that Chef just happened to have in her car and let us borrow.

"It seems like you really have found your niche, Jennifer," Dad said, as he bit into a tiny square of Opera Torte. Right before all the guests arrived, I had carefully written the word *Opera* on every small slice. My wrist felt sore to prove it.

"Yeah, it's a lot of fun, and I feel more at home here than in the regular Culinary Program," I said. I really did. When I looked back and thought that only two months ago I was breaking down chickens and deboning fish, I shuddered. Here, I was constantly surrounded by freshly baked bread, frosting in every color, and *petits fours*. Dad was right; I *did* feel like I had found my niche.

"There are more pastries across the hall," I told him, signaling into the next kitchen, which was a more advanced pastry class.

"This is just unreal!" Dad said as we passed rows and rows of perfect lemon tarts, miniature chocolate-chip cookies, and two-inch slices of flourless chocolate torte. In the next kitchen, there were *macarons* of every flavor and color: coconut, lime, licorice, chocolate, vanilla, peach, and rose. All were no larger than a quarter and were filled with bright, creamy fillings. I grabbed a coconut and rose *macaron* to sample, since I hadn't had anything to eat since dinner, and that was hours ago. Usually on school nights I packed a snack, such as a granola bar or some dried fruit and nuts, but tonight I had been too rushed to think of anything besides how to spell *Opera*.

As I bit into the rose *macaron*, I was transported right back to France. The exterior crackled on my tongue and tasted lightly of flowers and sugar-sweet perfume. Surprisingly, rose is a very popular flavor in France, and often it's paired with raspberry in candies and pastries. The *macaron* I was eating had a delicate raspberry jellylike filling that went perfectly with the crumbly rose cookie.

Raspberry-Rose Macarons

Makes about 18 macarons

Raspberry-rose is a traditional flavor combination in France, but if you'd rather make plain macarons, substitute the rose extract for vanilla and sandwich the cookies together with chocolate or vanilla buttercream frosting.

For the white chocolate-raspberry *ganache*
  4 ounces white-chocolate chips
  ¼ cup half-and-half or cream
  2 tablespoons raspberry jam (I use Bonne Maman)

For the cookies
  1 cup powdered sugar
  ½ cup ground almonds
  2 egg whites, room temperature
  5 tablespoons granulated sugar
  1 teaspoon rose extract
  1 drop red food coloring

First, make the *ganache* **filling:** Melt white chocolate and cream using a double boiler (or in a metal bowl set over a pot of simmering water). Whisk chocolate and cream together, breaking up any lumps. Add the jam and stir well. Push *ganache* through a fine-mesh strainer (I use a sifter) to get rid of the raspberry seeds. Let *ganache* cool for at least 2 hours at room temperature before using. It will thicken as it cools.

Preheat the oven to 350°F.

Make the cookies: Combine the powdered sugar and almonds in a bowl and mix well to combine. Using a stand mixer, whip the egg whites until foamy. Add the granulated sugar, rose extract, and food coloring and continue to whip until stiff, glossy peaks form. In two batches, fold in the powdered sugar and almond mixture. Scrape batter into a pastry bag with a ¼-inch pastry tip, and pipe out tablespoon-size mounds of batter onto a lined baking sheet.

Bake the *macarons* for 12 minutes. Let cool completely, then peel *macarons* off baking sheet.

When cookies are totally cool, spread a teaspoon or so of white chocolate–raspberry *ganache* on half the cookies, and sandwich with the other half.

Blood Orange Tarts

Makes four 3-inch individual tarts or one 8-inch tart

Save any extra curd from these tarts to spread on muffins and scones. The puckery taste and stunning color are wonderful.

For the blood orange curd
    Juice of one blood orange
    Juice of one lemon
    Zest of one lemon
    ½ cup sugar
    3 eggs, plus 1 egg yolk
    ½ stick (4 tablespoons) butter at room temperature,
        cut into small chunks

For the tart shells
    ¾ cup all-purpose flour
    1 tablespoon sugar
    Pinch of salt
    ½ stick (4 tablespoons) cold butter, cut into chunks
    1 egg yolk
    1 tablespoon whole milk or cream

Make the curd first so that it has ample time to chill and set in the refrigerator: Line a sheet tray with wax paper. Whisk together the blood orange juice, lemon juice, lemon zest, sugar, eggs, and egg yolk in a large heatproof bowl. Place the bowl over a pot of simmering water to make a double boiler and add the butter. Whisk continuously until the mixture begins to thicken, about 10 minutes, then, using a rubber spatula, continue to gently stir until the curd is thick and creamy and coats the back of the spatula completely. (This entire process will take about 15–20 minutes.) Once the curd is thick, take it off the heat and pour onto the wax paper–lined sheet tray, spreading it thin. Press a piece of plastic wrap on top of the curd to cover it completely and transfer to the refrigerator for an hour to set.

Preheat the oven to 375°F.

Make the tart shells: Mix together the flour, sugar, and salt. Cut in the butter with your fingertips until the mixture resembles sand. Add the yolk and cream and combine until mixture forms a ball.

Knead the dough until a smooth dough forms. Roll out the dough on a floured surface and press it into greased mini-tart shells. You could also roll out the dough and press it into a pie dish. Prick dough with a fork. Bake the shells or pie shell until slightly golden, about 20 minutes. Remove from the oven and let cool completely.

Fill the tart shells (or pie) with the curd and transfer to the refrigerator for at least 8 hours to set completely.

13

PIECE OF CAKE

WEDDING CAKE CLASS STARTED OFF PAINFULLY. Granted, I was assigned to be in a group with Samantha and Jake, and it was fun to work with friends, spending the late evenings laughing and making fondant, sugar roses, and Styrofoam cake layers. But the class quickly cemented my sense that I had no knack whatsoever for decorating cakes, not to mention zero patience. It made me almost miss the crazy, fast-paced mess of Basic Skills I, where I'd at least been able to release some stress by chopping and sautéing; in Wedding Cakes, I felt stifled and awkward. To make matters worse, I realized just how artistic some of the other students in the class were, including Samantha.

"See? You just gently twirl the cake stand while you squeeze icing from your other hand," she said, trying to show me how to make a buttercream rose for the second time. As hard as I tried, I couldn't seem to spin the stand and form the creamy rose petals at the same time. I always just ended up with a blob of frosting melting all over my fingers. It was hopeless, and maddening.

"I can't get it!" I said, gritting my teeth in frustration. This wasn't just about the buttercream roses. I'd always thought of myself as a good cook and baker, someone who was good with her hands and thoughtful in the kitchen. Someone who *got it*. These buttercream roses made me wonder if I was really cut out for any of this. I felt defeated.

Samantha already had seven perfect buttercream roses sitting on tiny pieces of wax paper in front of her. Jake, on the other hand, was more on my level and at that moment was discussing his plight with Chef Matthews. I shifted around on my bar stool and picked up the pastry bag once again. I never thought I would rather be cutting meat than frosting cakes, but this was getting ridiculous.

"What did your wedding cake look like?" I asked Samantha, while picking pieces of dried frosting out from underneath my fingernails.

She laughed. "Well, you know we got married at Disney, right? The cake was a big pumpkin, like the one from Cinderella! Vanilla cake and lots of buttercream. It was perfect."

On the outside I smiled, but on the inside I felt like I was about to die laughing. Living in Orlando had introduced me to the subculture of Disney World "groupies." Every day on my drive to school, I saw them all dressed as their favorite characters, boarding buses into the park. Samantha was a great girl, but she was one of those groupies, and sometimes I questioned her taste.

In my mind, a wedding cake should be tall and white with lots of delicate frosting swirls. Not that I was offering to make one—that seemed like a clear recipe for disaster. But at the end of the night, that's exactly what Chef Matthews told us we had to do. Each of us would make a wedding cake—no partners on this assignment—for the last night of class. It would be worth exactly half of our total grade. I was doomed.

When I got home it was close to 12:30 a.m. Every time I took a step, my black rubber clogs squeaked from a glob of frosting that had spread out on the soles. The wedding cake project already was looming over my head, even though it wasn't due for two and half weeks. I had no clue what I would do or what it would look like. Paging through wedding magazines had never been one of my priorities. I flopped down on my queen-size bed and debated calling Rob to say goodnight but then remembered what time it was. Lately, our conversations had been shorter than before due to my school schedule and his job. But that was normal, I told myself. We had been dating for so long that we didn't need to have deep, hour-long conversations late at night when we were both already exhausted. Rob with his fishing, rum and Cokes, and good-natured laughter. We were opposites in every way possible, yet somehow we still managed to make things work.

The next night in school, I sat with Samantha and Jake in the computer lab doing "research" on different wedding cake styles. Not too surprisingly, Samantha had chosen a gothic Halloween theme for her cake and was busy finding patterns of skulls and crossbones online to copy onto her cake. Like me, Jake had no idea what he wanted his cake to look like yet, and the two of us spent the hour goofing off instead of researching like we were supposed to. Jake was an interesting guy, and I enjoyed getting to know him. He was incredibly intelligent and loved video games, baking bread, and physics. He was a geek, the kind who probably dresses up to go see Harry Potter movies. *Talking to him is a lot more fun than talking to most of Rob's friends*, I thought to myself.

"What about this one?" I asked Jake as I scrolled through a site of simple blue wedding cakes with cherry blossoms winding over the layers.

"That looks like it might be sort of difficult, but I love the colors!" Jake responded enthusiastically. *Hmmm*, I thought to myself. *How hard could this really be?*

In the kitchen the next day, we were handed rolls of white fondant. The fondant was soft and felt like pie dough made out of smooth clay. It smelled sweet, like frosting, and could be easily molded and cut into various shapes and sizes. I immediately pulled off a tiny edge of mine and brought it to my lips. There was no real flavor other than sugar, and it tasted intensely sweet. I chose to dye my fondant a robin's-egg blue, like the wedding cake I had seen on the Internet, and soon my palms had turned the same color. In my excitement to get started, I had forgotten the crucial step of wearing gloves while working with the food coloring. Blue dye sank into the lines of my hands and onto my short fingernails. *This will be interesting to explain to Tony tomorrow at work*, I thought. But I kept squeezing my fondant, which was now swirled blue and white, to get an even color before I attempted to cover my first cake layer. I had decided to go with a completely blue cake and then, despite Jake's doubts, make a rather intricate cherry-blossom pattern winding up from the base. I thought it would be interesting if nothing else.

The next day I rushed from work to school with bright blue hands and a new sense of determination. Even though I knew that decorating cakes was not my strong suit, I wanted to prove to myself that I could do it. My blue fondant was waiting for me right where I'd left it, and I immediately began rolling it out with a large wooden rolling pin. After a few minutes of hard rolling, I had a large, smooth disk of fondant in front of me. I dotted the top of my first Styrofoam layer with glue and neatly laid the fondant on top. I still found it ironic that we were using Styrofoam and glue to decorate wedding cakes. For the sake of time, we weren't actually baking the cakes that we were decorating. I'd initially felt a little let down when I heard that, but I realized that it made sense to focus on the decorating aspect instead of more baking. Still, the whole process seemed more like a child's arts and crafts project than an advanced class at Le Cordon Bleu.

I kept rolling and working with my fondant for the next hour, until small beads of sweat dotted my eyebrows and my neck, where my cravat remained tied tight. There were still air bubbles around the sides of the layers, bubbles that no matter how hard I tried, I couldn't seem to smooth out. Every time I smoothed one, another one would pop up right next to it. Feeling frustrated and hungry, I grabbed my snack of a homemade oatmeal cookie and fled to the hallway to eat in peace. I had baked these cookies for Rob and my brother last weekend when I was home in Tampa, and I'd taken a few home with me for late-night school snacks. They were pretty healthy, really, and contained flaxseeds, almond butter, and dark-chocolate chips. Come to think of it, I probably liked them a lot better than the boys did.

After taking my time eating my cookie, checking my voicemail, and stopping by the hallway water fountain, I made my way back inside the cool classroom kitchen. All seventeen students were working diligently on their cakes, and as a result, the room was almost silent. Back at my table, Samantha had her headphones on and was deep in concentration. In the time it took me to wrap my three Styrofoam layers alone, she had already begun working on the meticulous border of ghoul faces that wrapped around every layer of her cake. Jake, on the other hand, was still trying to cover his pieces and looked just as frustrated as I'd felt all evening.

"How's it goin' over here, guys?" Chef Matthews asked as he suddenly appeared at the end of our table.

"Pretty good," I responded, trying to stay positive. "I'm almost ready to start the cherry-blossom pattern on my cake." Chef nodded and glanced at Samantha, who was still working away, most likely while listening to a Disney soundtrack.

"Samantha?" Chef asked, inches from her face.

She grew beet red. "I'm sorry, Chef! I was totally absorbed in this. Did you say something?" she asked.

"I'd rather you not have headphones on in class. It makes it hard for me to direct the entire class as one body. I thought I mentioned that the first night we met."

"I'm sorry. It won't happen again, Chef. I honestly didn't realize." Samantha stuffed her iPod into her backpack and smiled sweetly up at him. Chef just nodded and moved on to the next table.

Once he was gone, Samantha sighed dramatically. "I can't believe he won't even let us listen to music! Decorating cakes is all about artistic passion. How are we expected to let that passion out when we can't get in our zone?"

For the rest of the evening we worked in silence, and by the time 11:30 rolled around, I had made a batch of brown fondant and begun cutting it into thin ropes to serve as my cherry-blossom branches. The cake still wasn't as smooth as I had hoped, but it was turning out just fine. On the way home, my cell phone buzzed and Rob's face lit up my caller ID. *What in the world is he doing up so late?* I wondered before answering.

"I was just thinking about you. I love you, Jenna," Rob's smooth voice filled my ears and brought a smile to my face.

"I love you, too," I said and meant it. Rob made life so easy, stable, and predictable. While many of my friends from college were hanging out in bars looking for a date, I had found security and stability in my relationship. And here in Orlando, I felt I had the best of both worlds. I could maintain my space and independence, with an apartment and friends of my own, and still go back on the weekends and enjoy time with my boyfriend. I've always needed plenty of alone time, and that made this situation work out nicely. Rob and I still rarely spoke about the future, other than discussing whose engagement parties and weddings we were scheduled to be at in the upcoming weeks, but when we were together we enjoyed each other's company as much as ever.

The next day was filled with final wedding-cake adjustments. I planned to use the first two hours of class to finish adhering the cherry blossoms to my cake, and the last three hours to pipe icing borders and do any last finishing touches. Though the cakes weren't due at the end of class, it was the last class period that Chef Matthews was giving us to work on them before we moved on to our written exam the following night. Samantha's cake was already finished, and it stood eerily on its pedestal at the front of the classroom. Even though the creepy theme really wasn't my personal favorite, I had to admit that the final outcome was nothing short of stunning. The entire cake was a rich, deep purple, with delicate orange ghoul faces at the base of every layer. She had made skull-and-crossbones cutouts with *pastillage*, a sugary dough that hardens like cement when it dries. I, too, had dabbled in the world of *pastillage*, but only to make a simple heart shape. After I applied my last bit of royal icing, I stood back a few feet from my cake to evaluate it. The cake looked good, despite a slight tilt to the left and some leftover air bubbles in my fondant that I hadn't been able to pound out. The cherry-blossom pattern was, hands down, my favorite part, and I loved the way it flowed up the cake. I had had a little trouble molding the small blossoms, but they ended up turning out just fine, and I was proud of my work. The only problem was that it was inedible. The recipe below for flourless choco-late cake is a much more delicious option.

Flourless Chocolate Cake with Vanilla-Buttercream Frosting

Makes two 9-inch cake layers

Keep this cake in mind when you want to pamper yourself or another serious chocolate lover. I like to store the cake in the fridge and serve cold slices with espresso.

For the cake
10 ounces (about 2 cups) semisweet chocolate
5 ounces butter
6 eggs, at room temperature
½ cup granulated sugar

For the frosting
2 sticks (½ pound) butter, softened
2 cups confectioner's sugar
1 tablespoon milk
2 teaspoons vanilla extract

Preheat the oven to 350°F. Thoroughly butter two 9-inch cake pans, then dust each lightly with flour and set aside.

Make the cake layers: In a small saucepan over very low heat, melt chocolate and butter together. While mixture is melting, whip eggs in a stand mixer at high speed. After about 3 minutes, when eggs start to become thick and pale, add sugar slowly. Continue whipping on high until the mixture is thick, pale, and ribbony, about 6–8 more minutes.

Slowly fold melted chocolate into the egg-and-sugar mixture, gently turning with a rubber spatula so that batter stays light and airy. Pour batter into cake pans.

Bake for 30 minutes, then remove from oven and let cool in cake pans for 10 minutes. Run a knife around edges of cakes and transfer from pans onto a wire rack to cool completely.

While cakes are cooling, make the frosting: In the bowl of a stand mixer, beat butter and sugar together until combined. Add milk and vanilla extract, and continue beating on high until the frosting is thick and light, about 5 minutes.

When the cake layers are cooled completely, spread one third of the frosting on top of one layer, and top with the other layer. Frost top and sides of cake with remaining frosting.

14
THE CLAW

O N THE FIRST DAY OF CAPSTONE CLASS, I WAS FULL OF anticipation and nervous energy. This was the final course in the Baking and Pastry program before we went off on our externships—stints working in real, professional kitchens and bakeries. This class would dictate if we were cut out to go. We had been working toward Capstone all year; it was the goal, the finale that tested all of the skills we had been drilled on for the past ten months. Unlike in other classes, no books were allowed here—we were to rely on the diligent notes taken in previous classes, and recipes we'd written out on three-by-five note cards. As part of the class curriculum, we would be preparing at least one dish using each technique we'd studied, and all of our dishes would be graded on a very strict universal Cordon Bleu scale. There would be no sweet-talking our way into better grades, and certainly no cutting corners.

The next few days would set apart the chefs from the ordinary culinary students and determine our success in the whole program. The pressure felt like rocks on my chest. There was no room for error here; if we didn't get something right, we couldn't just try to do better next time. Next time would be an actual restaurant kitchen with a boss and prep cooks on the line. This was our last chance to work with instructors, our last chance to learn from our mistakes rather than get fired for them.

I glanced over at my friends, who were sitting silently, staring straight ahead. Part of me wanted to cry while part of me wanted to let out a loud *whoop* at the utter hilarity of taking something like baking croissants so seriously. I took my place at the cold metal counter and dug in my bag for my note cards and lip balm. The night before I had stayed up late studying the syllabus and creating a timeline for what to bake when, to ensure that everything would have enough time and room in the oven. The syllabus had been short, only one page, and had simply listed in alphabetical order the items we were to bake during the week. It was up to us to manage our time efficiently. As stressful as it was, I actually enjoyed the extra responsibility because it made class seem more like a job and less like school.

I chose to make the four required pastries first—bear claws, *palmiers*, *vol au vents* (simple jam-filled Danishes), and a buttery French almond pastry called a *pithivier*—because there were my least favorites, and also because they required the most preparation time. The blitz puff pastry used in all four products had to be prepared a day ahead of time so that it could have a slow, cold rise in the walk-in fridge overnight. I planned to start my sponge cake after prepping all the dough.

All at once it seemed my classmates were grabbing flour, butter, and yeast from various shelves at a rapid pace, but I chose to hold back and do things a little more slowly than the rest. I got my butter from the walk-in fridge and started chopping the thick slices into small chunks for my puff pastry dough. Every time I had made puff pastry dough in the past, the sheer amount of butter that went into it always flabbergasted me. It felt therapeutic, though, leaning up against a giant mixer and throwing cold chunks of butter in one by one for about twenty minutes. My dough was forming quite nicely and, when it was finished mixing, I took it out and gently wrapped it in plastic wrap to set in the fridge for half an hour. Then, I would perform the first fold, which basically meant just folding more butter on top of the dough and sealing the edges shut. Traditionally, when preparing classic puff pastry dough, bakers fold the dough dozens of times in a process known as laminating.

The next night I came in ready to roll (no pun intended). I had a lot of pastries to make from that one slab of dough, and I was determined to get done and get my station cleaned up by 9:30, so I could go home early. After grabbing my hunk of dough from the walk-in, I began working on the *pithiviers* because making them was by far the most dreaded task. *Pithiviers* consist of two circles of puff pastry with a mound of almond paste in the center, sort of like a giant toaster strudel. They are incredibly tasty, for sure, but they can prove to be disastrous if the edges of the pastry aren't sealed completely. All of my previously attempted *pithiviers* had exploded in the deck oven. So tonight I made a big deal out of pressing down the dough very, very firmly and putting extra egg wash on top to make it extra shiny. I placed them in the oven then ran back to my station to form my *vol au vents* and bear claws.

Everything was going smoothly. For the first time, my *pithiviers* did not explode, and my *vol au vents* looked close to perfect. I felt excitement well up as I looked proudly at the pastries surrounding me. *Three down, one to go*, I thought, then eagerly started on my bear claws. Around 8:45, however, after forming, shaping, and proofing my dough, I noticed that there was a bit of a size discrepancy between my bear claws and those of my classmates. Mine were the size of baseball gloves, while everyone else's were the size of my palm. I felt a sense of dread come over me as I carefully applied a second layer of egg wash to the proofed dough before shutting the bear claws inside the oven. I didn't have enough time or dough to remake the claws, so all I could do was stand in front of the oven and watch them grow. To my dismay, as the clock ticked on, my bear claws progressively got larger and larger. I excused myself to take a walk to the bathroom to burn off some nervous energy while assuring myself that this wasn't the end of the world. *Surely* I wasn't going to fail the program based on giant pastries alone.

A few deep yoga breaths later, I was back in the kitchen, pulling my sheet pan out of the oven and setting all my pastries together to be graded. My *pithiviers* looked amazing, the best I had ever done, as did my *vol au vents* and *palmiers*. But those bear claws were as large as a grown man's head. I pulled a marker out of my coat pocket to label my products and decided the best way to go about this was to use humor to my advantage. I wrote in big, swirly handwriting, "PAPA BEAR'S CLAWS." It was hard to get a smile out of Chef Horn, who also happened to be the dean of the Baking and Pastry program, but I figured it was worth a shot. I took my sheet tray and stuck it in the rack with everyone else's products. After we were gone for the evening, Chef would look at all the pastries and grade everyone; we'd have to wait until the end of the week to see our scores.

Turned out, Chef must have seen the humor in the situation because much to my disbelief, I actually scored high on my bear claws and other pastries. I let out a big sigh of relief that Capstone was finally over. As much as I prided myself on thriving under pressure, I was ready to relax and soak up my final days in Orlando before packing up again. I felt a great sense of accomplishment over what I had done, failures and all, and was ready to move on.

15

GOING HOME AGAIN

FINALLY, THE DAY CAME TO SAY GOOD-BYE. THOUGH IT WASN'T my first choice, in the end I decided to move back to my home-town of Vero Beach to do my baking externship at a yacht club only two miles away from the house where I grew up. Originally, I had wanted to go out west, maybe to a spa in California or Arizona, but I got offered a good temporary position back home that I couldn't turn down. Plus, it was much more affordable than taking off and moving across the country for only three months. I told myself that California could wait. Instead, I planned on staying at the home of the parents of my best friend from high school for the next few months. They had generously offered me their guest room while Christie was away at law school, and from my window I had a view of the river that we spent so many Saturdays jet-skiing on as teenagers.

I knew that Rob was more than a little upset that I hadn't chosen to do my externship at a restaurant in Tampa where he had connec-tions, but I promised that after these three months I would finally move there to be with him. As I packed up my apartment in Orlando and cleaned out my closet, I paused to look at photographs and recipes that had accumulated on my top shelf over the past year, along with books, books, and more books. Since Helen had moved out a few months back, I had spread out my things all over the apartment, which I now considered my own. I hadn't seen or spoken to Helen at all during the past two months, but that was normal for us when we were apart. Helen and I had one of those rare close friendships that could just pick up right where it left off, no matter how much time and distance came between us.

"We've got our work cut out for us!" Rob exclaimed when he arrived at the apartment to help me move. Lamps, kitchen utensils, and books lay scattered on the living room floor, along with a few open suitcases and book boxes. All of the furniture was Helen's, and she had a mover coming the next day to take care of everything, so I just had to gather up all my things and hit the road.

"I already put some stuff in my car," I said, running my fingers through my hair, which I'd cut short in preparation for my externship. "Are you hungry?" I asked. "I just got back from a run and I'm starved."

"Always hungry! Let's just carry some of this stuff down now on our way out and we'll get something to eat," Rob said.

We had a nice dinner with glasses of red wine at the grill down the street. Rob stuck to pizza, which was personal size and Chicago style, cheese oozing over the sides of the crust and into the deep-dish pan. Pieces of pepperoni and sausage lay nestled in the cheese, a stark contrast to my grilled salmon and broccoli. After we ate, we headed back to the house to finish packing. That night, as I lay on my mattress on the floor in the empty apartment, worried thoughts filled my mind. Was I choosing the easy road or the road less traveled? I could start to see my future laid out in front of me, and it scared me a bit. I would most likely do my externship, move back to Tampa, take a safe job, and settle down and get married within the next year. I wondered if my dream of exploring California would ever actually come true. Finally, the thoughts seemed to settle in my head and I fell into a dark, dreamless sleep on that mattress, preparing myself for what was to come.

The next morning I had pretty much packed all my food except for staples like flour, milk, and baking powder. I used those to make us a big plate of soft, doughy pancakes as fuel for the trip. Though it was only eight in the morning, it was already a scorcher outside, the sun blazing bright in the Orlando sky. Rob was starting to lug my suitcases down the two flights of stairs while I wrapped up all the bedding into a big ball before stuffing it into a large suitcase.

It was my brilliant idea to just bungee-cord my mattress to the top of the car and drive it home—about 60 miles across the state of Florida. Rob was skeptical but willing, so we secured it as best we could and hit the road. I waved good-bye to my old apartment and headed west to Tampa. We got a few strange looks and honks because of the mattress, but we only had to pull over once to adjust it a bit tighter.

Rob was a trouper through it all, helping me unpack and temporarily housing all my books until I moved back in December. I spent the night with my family in Tampa, and the next day I headed out early in the morning for Vero Beach. People always say there's nothing like the feeling of going home, and as I drove my beat-up black Honda over the bridge that connected the mainland to the island where I grew up, I felt a surge of gratitude for this place and this time in my life. I rolled down my window, inhaled the rich saltwater air, and blasted old CDs from high school that reminded me of beach parties and tanning on the school football field during lunch breaks.

Vero Beach was a small town, the type of place you go on vacation when you're older and living time zones away. The town has two high schools and a small shopping center, the main attraction being the beach, which is known both for great surf and for shark sightings. I had always been so anxious to get out of that town, to make something of myself, and not become one of the "townies" who never left Vero after graduating high school. As teenagers, Christie and I used to sit on her dock facing the Indian River and talk about where we would be five years down the road. I was the one who got voted "first to marry," as I had always found myself in serious relationships with guys who wanted to settle down. Really, though, all I wanted was to write books, and I had always hoped my five-year plan involved a novel, not a husband.

Now, coming back five years later, I wondered how much had really changed. I certainly wasn't married yet, and although I had always jotted down in my journal funny anecdotes about things that had happened at school, there was no national bestseller in my immediate future. I pulled into Christie's driveway and greeted her parents with big hugs before they helped me drag my luggage up to their guest room. Betty, Christie's mom, had prepared a delicious meal celebrating my arrival; we ate grilled salmon and drank white wine with the door open and the gentle beach breeze blowing in and through my hair. It felt odd to sit at their dining room table without my friend next to me, and I wished that she were there to laugh with me and ease my anxious nerves about starting my externship.

Betty's salmon was perfectly cooked and topped with a Mediterranean tapenade made from tomatoes, pine nuts, olives, and feta. We ate it with creamy polenta studded with rich gorgonzola cheese and garlic, and roasted green beans on the side. After dinner, I headed to bed early to make sure I got enough sleep for my first day in the kitchen. I forgot how silent it was there at night, with only the sound of the river gently lapping outside, and fell asleep almost instantly.

In the days and weeks that followed, I slowly grew accustomed to working in a kitchen, rather than just trying to make the grade at school. I was pretty used to being the only girl on the line, but knew it wasn't easy to work under pressure with a bunch of guys. Luckily, I worked under the head pastry chef and was usually able to get most of my baking done in the early morning, so my hours weren't extremely late. It felt great to have my evenings back and free. At the club we made everything in house, from the rolls served in the breadbasket to the pie crust. I liked everyone I worked with, and just as I had at school, I loved baking bread the best. Seeing that my interest was piqued, the pastry chef had me experiment with new recipes and formulas, and soon I was not only whipping out two hundred rolls by 8 a.m. but also coming up with ideas of my own.

It was fall, and we were gearing up for Thanksgiving—the club's biggest holiday, since it was smack-dab in the middle of prime tourist season in Vero Beach. Everything was pumpkin; we had pumpkin bread constantly in the oven, pumpkin crème brûlée on the dessert menu, and pumpkin cheesecake in the fridge. I had recently become fascinated with the concept of the Whoopee Pie—billowy buttercream frosting sandwiched in between two large soft cookies—and thanks to the freedom that Chef had given me to experiment, I developed a Pumpkin Whoopee Pie that went over well with him and our clientele.

Even though the majority of our members were older, they actually loved the concept and welcomed Whoopee Pies as a change of pace from the chocolate and macadamia cookies that were always found on the dessert tray. For the big Thanksgiving Day buffet, I was in charge of baking the breads and making my Pumpkin Whoopee Pies.

I actually enjoyed getting to work early in the morning to start on the breads, when it was all quiet and dark outside and I could sip my coffee and sink my palms deep into the dough. Even though decorating wasn't my favorite, I loved to watch Chef work on intricate wedding cakes and *petits fours*, amazed at the details his large hands could master, when my tiny hands couldn't even make a proper chocolate garnish. He didn't give up on me, though, and whenever it was slow after lunch, I would retreat to the back office with a piece of wax paper and a metal bowl full of perfectly tempered chocolate that I would pour into a parchment-paper cone and attempt to drizzle in little patterns.

It was also nice being back in Vero Beach. I found myself getting back into running in my extra time and enjoyed sunny jogs down by the bridge and near the Indian River, where I had spent countless sunny weekend afternoons water-skiing and boating. Also, I didn't cut or burn myself nearly as much as I had while in school. I slowed myself down and was hell-bent on showing all the boys that they weren't the only ones who could make it in the kitchen.

Time flew by that fall, and before I knew it, I was packing up yet again, but this time for a final destination: Tampa. My graduation would be held in early December. I was looking forward to being closer to my family and finally attempting a normal relationship with

Rob, instead of dealing with the miles between us. Culinary school had seemed like a dream, hazy and sweet and over too soon. With my degree I now had the tools to take on any kitchen, any bakery; however, I wasn't sure why I still felt so unsettled. I packed up all my tools and neatly folded my uniforms and drove west, away from my tiny hometown, feeling prepared to take on new experiences as a culinary school graduate. New Year's Eve was spent at a bar in South Tampa, and I cheered and toasted with Rob and our friends to 2009, the last year in the decade and a year for new possibilities and growth. If I only knew then how much growth the year would really bring.

Pumpkin Whoopee Pies

Makes about 18 whoopee pies

These cookies are very rich, almost like a cupcake, so I suggest saving this recipe for a special occasion or a rainy afternoon. The cookies are best the day you bake them; if you keep them for too long they will become a bit gummy and soft. They would also be perfect with cream cheese frosting in the middle, or on their own, sprinkled with a dusting of powdered sugar.

For the buttercream filling
   1 egg white
   2 tablespoons milk
   1 teaspoon vanilla extract
   2 cups powdered sugar, divided
   ¾ cup shortening

For the cookies
   2 cups brown sugar
   1 cup canola oil
   1½ cups canned pumpkin
   2 eggs
   1 teaspoon vanilla extract
   3 cups all-purpose flour

1 teaspoon salt
1 teaspoon baking powder
1 teaspoon baking soda
1½ teaspoons cinnamon
½ teaspoon cardamom
¼ teaspoon ground cloves
¼ teaspoon ground white pepper
1½ teaspoons ground ginger

Make the filling: In the bowl of a stand mixer fitted with a whisk attachment, combine the egg white, milk, vanilla extract, and 1 cup of the powdered sugar, then mix on high speed until the mixture is creamy and light. Add shortening and remaining cup of sugar, and whip on high speed until very light, about 8 to 10 minutes. Set aside.

Preheat the oven to 325°F. and line a baking sheet with parchment paper.

Make the cookies: In a large bowl, blend together brown sugar and oil with a spoon until well combined. Add pumpkin, eggs, and vanilla and continue to stir until smooth.

Sift together flour, salt, baking powder, baking soda, and spices, and then add to the wet ingredients, stirring only until combined (be careful not to overmix).

For best results, spoon batter into a piping bag with a large tip and pipe mounds of batter (about 1 tablespoon each) of batter onto the lined sheet tray, about 3 inches apart. (If you don't have a piping bag, use two large spoons and space the batter in the same way.)

Bake cookies for about 10–12 minutes, until they begin to turn golden. Let cool completely before sandwiching cookies together with the filling.

Cookie sandwiches will keep in a sealed plastic container at room temperature for a few days.

16

NIGHT AND DAY

Two months later

AWOKE WITH A START AND SLAMMED MY HAND DOWN ON THE alarm clock by my bedside. I had been dreaming again of Paris, of making my way through the farmers' markets and winding Latin Quarter streets. The red digital numbers read 3:01 a.m., and I had to be at work by four.

I stepped out of bed and made my way down the carpeted hallway to the bathroom, rubbing my eyes. I had these early mornings down to a science. I knew that it took exactly one minute to get from bed to bathroom, four minutes to quickly rinse off in the shower, five minutes to get dressed, and another six minutes to make a snack and coffee for the drive to work.

I washed my face, brushed my teeth, and checked my watch to make sure I was still going on time. Hot coffee with agave nectar and a little half-and-half was next, plus a hard-boiled egg and a piece of cheese to keep me going until around eight o'clock, when I could take my break to eat a full breakfast.

As usual, the store parking lot was dark, and I rang the bell at the side entrance to have my manager come let me in. When the sliding glass doors opened I was ushered into a whole new world. Stockers were already busy unloading boxes of cereal and crackers, and crates of produce were coming in through the back door. I quickly tied on my apron and got to work. All of the pastries had to be baked and shelved by the time the store opened at eight, and by that time all the bread had to be rising as well. Several buckets of sourdough starter had already been pulled out of the walk-in and were sitting on the wooden countertop, ready to be mixed with flour and water and shaped into artisanal breads. Here, I was a baker, and my main job was shaping dough into loaves and then firing them in five hundred-degree ovens. In the past couple of weeks, I had acquired some new scars on both forearms from wielding scalding-hot, industrial-size sheet pans.

Most mornings, there were two other people working in the bakery with me. We rarely spoke in the early hours as we piped commercially prepared raspberry and cherry fillings into puff pastry, pausing only to take long sips of steaming coffee. There were chocolate croissants to bake, as well as Danishes, bagels, muffins, and cookies. We didn't actually make any of these breakfast pastries from scratch; they came into the store already frozen from a reputable distributor, and my only job was to pull them apart in their frozen state and bake them. Usually I would sneak a chocolate chip or two while I worked.

By the time the store opened and the first customers walked in, I had the first loaves of bread out of the oven and was up to my elbows in vegan buttercream frosting, a recipe I'd created and that seemed to be a huge hit. All of our bread was organic and baked from scratch using house-made starters (fermented mixtures of flour and water that act as a natural form of yeast). The only one we didn't make by hand was the sourdough starter, and that was shipped in from San

Francisco, where the tradition of sourdough began hundreds of years before. We made white, whole wheat, nine-grain, sourdough, and sunflower-flax breads, and wonderfully crusty French baguettes. My favorite of all the breads we made was the dense, dark sunflower-flax. It was smaller than the rest of the loaves because the organic whole-wheat flour that we used produced a denser final product. The bread was filled with seeds and sweetened with a little honey; it was perfect to dunk into a bowl of hot soup or cover with creamy goat cheese and juicy tomato slices.

The sourdough was great as well, but fickle as only sourdough bread can be. The starter needed a lot of love, and whether the bread turned out or not depended mainly on the weather outside and the time the dough spent in the industrial-size Kitchen Aid. When perfect conditions prevailed, the bread rose up tall and firm and had a rich, almost cheesy taste to it. When the Tampa mornings were warm and thick with tropical humidity, the rising dough would often crumple into itself, producing a final product that was dimpled and marked with imperfection. Sometimes, we would throw a handful of toasted walnuts or hazelnuts into the dough when it was being mixed to form a sandwich roll reminiscent of the little hazelnut rolls I'd loved so much while in France.

I'd taken this baking job at a local organic supermarket for many reasons. The economy was crashing and burning, my school loan payments were about to start coming due, and the idea of baking bread just seemed fun. I got hired after my first interview, and I was so thrilled by the fact that I had even gotten a job that I accepted it in a heartbeat, only half-listening when they told me about the early-morning hours. I told myself it wouldn't be that big a deal, and that plenty of people worked early shifts. I still wanted to be a writer but figured I had to put in my time like everyone else before I could land my dream job at *Bon Appétit* or *Gourmet*. When I told my parents, they were happy that I'd gotten a job but worried about the low pay and my sleeping schedule. My dad hung blackout curtains in my bedroom and gave me a pep talk while my brother made bets on how long I would last.

On my first day of work, I arrived with an extra-large Thermos of black coffee, oatmeal in my lunchbox for my 8 a.m. "lunch break," and dark circles under my eyes. I had only slept for four hours. I didn't think about how difficult it would be to fall asleep while the sun was still in the sky and before a normal dinner time.

None of my friends could fathom why I had accepted a job working from 4 a.m. to noon every day for ten dollars an hour. I tried to reason with them, and with my family, who bore the brunt of my lack of sleep. I told everyone who asked that it was totally normal for a culinary school graduate to have a job at the low end of the totem pole and that baking bread from scratch was just *soooo* rewarding. Plus, it would give me a lot of time to work on my writing.

Compared to my externship in a somewhat high-stress kitchen, kneading bread in the middle of the night had sort of a romantic appeal to it. But in reality I ran around like a madwoman, wanting to do it all; after getting home from work at lunchtime I would hit the gym or the pool for a long swim or head out for a run before eating dinner at four and hitting the sack by seven. My goal was just to exhaust myself so much during the daytime that I couldn't help but fall asleep early enough to get a reasonable seven hours of sleep before waking up, writing for a few hours, and going to work again.

Let's just say that never happened. Not even close. What did happen was that I became painfully aware of what it feels like to have insomnia, to go to work feeling like a zombie all day with five hundred–degree air hitting me in the face. The upside to all this was the lack of need for makeup and hairstyling (hairnets took care of frizz and grease better than hairspray) and the plethora of delicious carbohydrates. Every afternoon I would come home with a new loaf of fresh-baked bread, my favorite being the potato bread, which had a texture so soft that it fell apart like cotton candy in your mouth and a flavor that just begged to be paired with crunchy almond butter and raspberry jam.

As the days wore on, however, I became more and more sleep deprived. My exhaustion made me less careful with scalding-hot sheet pans, and I acquired a new set of burns all over my arms. I had no motivation to exercise and made no progress on the writing front. Rob was increasingly perturbed because I never had the energy to go out with our friends anymore. I also started to have major issues falling asleep at night because I would just lie in bed and stare at the clock, fretting as I counted the dwindling hours until my alarm would ring. I had just begun and already knew something had to give.

One Friday evening, Rob and I were once again arguing over plans. In the whole three years that we had been dating, we'd never argued like this. A bunch of his friends were all going to a steakhouse in town, and he wanted us to go and then head downtown for drinks later. I had been up since three, and my eyelids had started to feel like they were being pulled together by magnets. All I wanted was a hot bubble bath and a good night's sleep; the thought of going out and being social almost seemed like a death sentence. No amount of eye makeup could mask the shadows around my eyes, and I could feel the crankiness start to set in.

"Babe, we haven't been out in over a month! I know you're tired, but can't we just compromise?" Rob asked.

I sighed. As much as I wanted to meet him halfway, I knew that once the cocktails started flowing there would be no going home early. Rob loved to have a good time, and even with the best intentions we would end up staying out until way past midnight. Then I would once again be the designated driver and responsible girlfriend.

"I honestly feel like I've been hit by a truck," I said. "Work was insane this morning, and I hardly slept at all last night. You go without me; it's not a big deal."

Rob looked hurt. "I don't *want* to go without you—you're my girl-friend. Most of the time we act like we're eighty years old and go to bed by ten. Can't you take a nap or something?"

In the end, Rob ended up going out alone. I really had nothing in common with any of his friends, and even though I knew it upset him, sometimes I liked it when he went out alone. I liked my personal time, when I could just read and write, rather than making small talk with his friends' wives, who already had kids and PTA meetings to deal with. Now, more than ever, I felt older than I really was, and I carried a sense of guilt because I knew I wasn't being fair to Rob. He would bend over backward to please me, and I was simply too tired to give him the same in return.

Back at my parents' house, I took a long bubble bath, then sank into my soft bed with a feeling of bliss that no steakhouse meal could ever have given me. All I wanted was to sleep before the cycle of early-morning alarm clocks, burning-hot ovens, and sweat began again.

Creamy Tomato Soup

Serves 4

My favorite way to enjoy a grilled cheese sandwich is to dunk it in this heavenly creamy soup. And, once you realize how easy it is to make, you'll never buy the canned version again. Just be sure to buy good quality diced tomatoes—it makes all the difference.

- 2 tablespoons butter
- ¼ yellow onion, finely chopped
- 2 tablespoons flour
- 2 cups diced tomatoes (or chopped fresh tomatoes in the summer)
- ¾ teaspoon sugar
- ¾ teaspoon salt
- ¼ teaspoon baking soda
- 2 cups whole milk

Heat the butter in a Dutch oven over medium-high heat, then add the onion and sauté until soft, about 5 minutes. Sprinkle the flour over the onion and toss well to combine. Cook for an additional 3 minutes, stirring often.

In a bowl combine the tomatoes with the sugar, salt, and baking soda and set aside.

Add the milk to the onion mixture, whisking, then whisk in tomato mixture. Bring to a simmer and continue to simmer for about 4 minutes (the soup will thicken up a little bit). Carefully pour the soup into a blender and blend until smooth, about 10 seconds.

Return soup to pot and keep warm over low heat until ready to serve.

17

WHEN EVERYTHING CHANGED

IT WAS THE END OF THE WEEK, AND ALL I COULD THINK ABOUT WAS getting my hair done. When it came to my appearance, I had pretty much stopped trying since I got the job at the bakery. In my oversized uniform without any makeup and my hair greased back into a hairnet-covered bun, I couldn't even recognize myself in the mirror. I certainly bore no resemblance to the perky blonde college girl who went shopping at J. Crew and Nordstrom on the weekends and stayed out late chatting over cocktails with girlfriends. But today I had an appointment with my stylist, and I couldn't wait to just sit back and let her work her magic on my overgrown roots and split ends. Since I had the weekend off, I was planning on meeting Rob and a couple friends for dinner later at a trendy new Mexican restaurant downtown.

I emerged from the salon feeling much more like my old self, and hurried home to change for the night.

"Helloooo?" I called out into my empty house, thinking maybe my brother was still upstairs where I'd left him a few hours before. I set my sunglasses and keys on the counter and swung the refrigerator door open to search for a late-afternoon snack, my freshly washed hair bouncing on my shoulders. I pulled out some leftover chicken to snack on before dinner. As I ate, my cell phone buzzed, and I answered it to chat with my mom, who had just landed in Albuquerque for work.

"Hang on, Mom," I said as the call-waiting light flashed. "Oh, never mind. It's just Dad calling on the other line. I'll call him back later."

We talked about weekend plans for a few seconds before my mom said, "Oh, that's funny, now he's calling me!"

"You can take the call if you want, Mom. I'm going to go take a quick nap anyway before meeting Rob in an hour."

"No, no . . . I'll call him back," she said, laughing. "He probably just wants to know what I left you guys for dinner. Tell me about your hair. Does it look cute?"

I could hear another phone ringing in the background and my mom's friend, Margaret, saying calmly, "Lynn, you better take this."

And then all I heard was screaming before the line went dead.

Panic bubbled in my chest and my hands started shaking. I instantly tried to call my mom back but the line was busy. The phone felt greasy and heavy in my hands, and then, all of a sudden, it was ringing and my dad's name flashed on the screen again.

"Dad? Is everything okay?" I asked immediately.

There was a brief moment of silence, and I could hear the strain of my father's breathing as he somehow found the words to tell me that my little brother had accidentally shot himself in the head and wasn't going to make it. The details were still sketchy, Dad said, but John had been over at a friend's house and somehow they'd been messing around with a gun when it accidentally went off in John's hands.

I left the house screaming, screaming, screaming. I screamed while grabbing my purse, my fist around the cold metal car keys, screamed while driving 65 miles an hour in a 40 zone down the road that John and I had jogged on together just one day earlier, screamed while searching frantically for a parking spot at the hospital, and screamed while running through the sliding glass doors of the emergency room. Somehow on the drive, I managed to call Rob. When I told him the news, he immediately left the golf tournament he was playing in and headed straight for Tampa General.

Once inside the hospital, I looked for the first person who seemed to work there and cried out, "My brother . . . John Weber . . . I got a call . . . is he here? He has to be here!"

"Miss, you need to calm down now. Take three deep breaths. There you go." The emergency room administrator turned to the man next to her and whispered something. "James will take you to your family now, Miss Weber. Follow him."

I started to cry then for the first time, hot tears flowing down my cheeks and dripping off my chin onto the hospital floor. Deliriously, I asked James how my brother could possibly be shot when he was laughing with his friends only a few hours ago. It wasn't right. It couldn't possibly be right. There had to be some mistake, the wrong kid or something. Didn't things like that ever happen? I thought I saw a movie once where it did. I was led into a tiny, dark room where my dad was hunched over a table, crying. I had never seen my dad cry before. I wondered how my mom was doing, 2,000 miles away.

"Jennifer. Oh, Jennifer," my dad cried, beating his fist on his thigh. "He's going to die. John is going to die."

The seconds, minutes, and hours that followed were all a blur but would leave jagged, sharp memories for years to come. My hand on my father's leg as he shook in pain, trying to be strong for me. Feeling my own legs buckle as I entered John's room in Intensive Care. Covering my mouth to control my screaming as Rob caught me in his arms.

We sat numbly all night in the waiting room as my mom made her way across the country, with two unavoidable layovers. In the end, John held on for eight hours after the shot. He was in no pain and never even heard the bang of the gun, since bullets travel faster than the speed of sound. As the heart monitor beeped to zero around 12:30 a.m., I put my hands on John's heart and felt his spirit leave. A chaplain came in and said Psalm 23 as I kissed my little brother's cold cheek good-bye.

I couldn't believe this was it. When we were growing up, we fought constantly. I was always the "good kid" with the good grades and gentle demeanor; John was the one who got busted throwing the wild parties, staying out too late, and speeding on the interstate. He lived life on the edge and got his thrills from pushing every limit set before him. He had a temper like no other, but at heart he was a good person. He had a soft spot for animals and the beach, often dragging his old surfboard across the street from our house to the ocean before the sun even started to rise in the sky. He would come home a few hours later, sandy and wet, and get ready to head to school, tracking sand into the shower and my car. A few summers earlier he had attempted to teach *me* how to surf, and while I caught a few waves, I was nowhere near as coordinated or stable on the board as he was.

The last thing I ever baked for John was banana bread. I poignantly remember him asking me if it was "normal" banana bread, meaning that most of the baked goods I made were too healthy for his liking. I lied and said yes, even though it was one hundred percent whole wheat and contained far less oil than the norm. John dug in as soon as the bread was done, not waiting for it to cool like I told him to. I joined him and we both cut thick slabs of the hot bread and burned our mouths together. After finishing his slice, John looked over at me and said, "Well, I guess it's good." My heart soared at that moment—I was so happy he'd enjoyed something I made. By the end of the night, the loaf of banana bread was gone.

My Brother's Favorite Banana Bread

Makes 1 loaf

Sliced and topped with honey, peanut butter, or raspberry jam, this sweet bread makes the best snack. Be sure to use only the ripest bananas here. You can ripen bananas quickly by storing them in a brown paper bag for a few days. And, you can keep any extra "black" bananas in the freezer for a few months.

- 3 large ripe bananas
- ½ cup organic cane sugar
- ¼ cup canola oil or melted coconut oil
- 2 tablespoons molasses
- 2 cups whole-wheat flour
- 1 teaspoon baking soda
- 1½ teaspoons cinnamon
- 1 teaspoon sea salt

Preheat the oven to 350°F. Spray a loaf pan with cooking spray.

Peel bananas and mash thoroughly in a medium-size bowl. Add sugar, oil, and molasses and stir well.

In a separate bowl, sift together dry ingredients, then gently fold into banana mixture. Pour into the prepared loaf pan and bake until golden brown, about 40 minutes.

Transfer loaf pan to a rack to cool for 15 minutes, then invert loaf onto rack.

18

JOHN'S GONE

OING HOME AFTER LEAVING THE HOSPITAL SEEMED surreal. How were we supposed to return to the dirty laundry and dishes in the sink like nothing ever happened? All I could do was focus on breathing, and even that felt labored and painful. I walked in the door, tossed my keys on the counter, and saw my empty plate with a few scraps of chicken on it from earlier that day lying in the sink. A few hours seemed like years. My throat felt swollen and my eyes burned from crying and exhaustion. Not knowing what to do next, despite the fact that it was nearly 2 a.m., I pulled out turkey from the fridge and made a sandwich on the sourdough bread I had baked the previous morning at work. Then, my dad's cell phone rang.

I spent the next two hours curled up in the wicker chair next to him as he spoke to the organ donation company that was about to harvest all of my little brother's organs. None of us could ever forget how he insisted on becoming an organ donor the day he got his driver's license. "Everybody's doing it at school!" he'd said, checking the box on the registration form.

As I absorbed the reality of John's death, it was hard not to feel cheated. Wasn't I, the older sister, supposed to die first? Wasn't that the natural order of the universe? I was an only child now, and John would never be there to take part in my wedding, be an uncle to my future kids, or help me take care of Mom and Dad when they grew old. Nothing about this made any sense. *Our lives were never meant to be this way*, I kept thinking.

When my mom finally walked through the front door at eight o'clock the next morning, she somehow looked as if she had lost ten pounds in one day. Her eyes were bright red and puffy, and she held a weak arm out for my father to support. I had made a fresh pot of coffee and poured her a steaming cup as my dad led her gently toward the couch.

"John's gone?" she mumbled, almost to herself. "Can I still see him? I need to say good-bye to my son!" My mom started wailing as only a mother who has just lost her child can do.

Somehow, I'd managed to get about an hour's worth of sleep the night before; I was still running on adrenaline despite the fact that I had been awake for nearly the past forty hours. I called John's high school principal to tell him the news. He answered the phone wearily, as if he had been up all night and expecting the call. When I told him, I could hear him start to cry, and he said he would come over to our house later with some food. Family began to arrive quickly, and I reunited with aunts, uncles, and cousins I hadn't seen in years. Our home was also filled with my brother's friends, mostly high school seniors, who sprawled out on our living room floor as they silently petted Mikan, my brother's dog, over and over.

I didn't cry much until the night after John's funeral. I was lying on Rob's couch, trying to numb my brain with an Oprah rerun, and suddenly tears started to stream down my cheeks.

"Jenna?" Rob called from the kitchen. "Do you want to go out for frozen yogurt or something?"

At that point, I was crying too hard to even form a sentence, and as he rushed to my side, I picked up my purse from the ground next to me and chucked it straight at the living room wall. The contents of the bag flew out and scattered on the floor while I sat sobbing, unable to move to pick anything up.

Not really knowing how to deal with me, Rob picked up my purse and gently led me down to the car and back to my parents' house, where I lay down in the dirt next to John's car and wailed. I wailed that his life had been cut so short, that we constantly fought when we were on earth together, that I wasn't there for him on the day he died. My mom and aunt held me as I sobbed, and when I was all cried out, the one thought that streamed through my mind over and over was that I couldn't go back to my middle-of-the-night baking job. I just couldn't go back. I didn't know why the thought was so strong, but it overtook me completely. For some time I had been feeling like something just had to give, and now it was giving. Big time.

So, the next morning, I called my boss and told him that due to the circumstances, I would not be returning. He was kind, of course, due to the circumstances. He also told me I was too valuable a worker to just let go, so for the next thirty days I would remain on payroll but not on the schedule. After a month, I could decide if I really wanted to quit or not. I told him this was completely unnecessary, that my mind was made up and I was incredibly sorry to put them in a bind. The idea of going back to work there was enough to make me scream; just the thought of the bakery sent my heart into panic mode.

The next few days after the funeral passed quickly, a hustle and bustle of airport trips, neighbors stopping by, and casseroles lining up centimeters apart on our kitchen counter. Most extended family had left the day after the service; only my aunt, my mother's sister, had remained to help out for a week. Though I finally had let go and cried, I still felt a hard ball of pain and anger in my chest that threatened to explode at any moment.

When it did, I was sitting on the couch with my mom and my aunt late in the afternoon. Rob and my dad were talking about hedge funds, and the news was droning softly on TV. My aunt was talking to my mom and me about how my twenty-something cousin had matured into such a great guy, and I laughed and said, "Well, I'm sure he's had his fair share of drinks and parties, too."

My aunt didn't smile but just turned to face me. "Nope. I would know. James never has touched marijuana before. He's a good guy."

"Are you telling me that my brother wasn't a good guy?" I asked, my face getting red and my heart starting to pound into my ears. Normally, I would never have started a conversation like this, but something in me just felt dark.

"Jennifer. I'm not saying Johnny wasn't *a good guy*. He was my godson, for crying out loud. I'm just saying my own son has never smoked pot before."

Something in me broke loose. "I know EXACTLY what you're saying. You're saying that your son was better than my brother and now my brother is dead. He is dead!" I started crying, getting madder and madder. "You know what, I hate you. I do. You're self-righteous and claim to live this perfect life with your perfect son

who never does anything wrong. I hate you, I hate you, I HATE YOU!"
I screamed.

I had no idea who I was in that moment. I ran out the door and slammed it. All I could hear now on the inside of the house was my mother wailing and my aunt sobbing. Had I done this? Had I just said such horrible, horrible things? I felt empty and alone. My brother was dead, I'd quit my job impulsively, and now I had just told my aunt that I hated her. *Hated* her. I'd never even thought such a thing before. She was my aunt, my mom's only sister—the same aunt who had changed my diapers, watched me grow up, and flown out from Wisconsin to watch me graduate from culinary school only a few months before. Too stubborn to go back inside, I sat at the end of our cobblestone driveway in the heat and dropped my head into my hands.

Where in the world was I supposed to go from here?

19

THE NEW NORMAL

E FILLED THE NEXT FEW WEEKS WITH ERRANDS; I DIDN'T want my mom to be by herself, and knew I had to keep myself busy to make it through. My aunt had left a few days after my outburst, and I had never apologized; instead I hid at Rob's house for the remainder of her stay. I was ashamed of my behavior, of course, but making things right with her had felt way too overwhelming. Living hour by hour was about all I could handle.

Physical activity became an outlet for my grief, but not in the way I would have expected. For the first time in my life, yoga scared me. Being vulnerable and open to discomfort in the way that yoga demands felt like it could suck the life out of me. The one time I attempted to go to my favorite Thursday-morning class, I almost had a panic attack and had to walk out while all the other students were sweating in triangles and plank poses. Instead, I took over John's elite membership at the health club down the street—the health club he often went to, after getting high with his friends, to sit in the steam room for hours on end. My dad had handed me John's membership card and told me it was mine now.

The first time I walked in the club to work out, I handed the cute brunette behind the front desk my brother's tattered card and she didn't understand.

"John Taylor Weber," she read aloud while smacking gum between her lips.

"Yeah . . . that's my brother," I said, not sure if I could say any more because my voice had started to give out and I felt a ball of emotion welling inside.

"Okay . . . if you are going to use his card I'm going to have to get you to fill out this form please. Is he out of town?" Smack, smack, smack went her pink gum. I grimaced.

"Well, actually he passed away last week." The words flew out of my mouth before I could stop them, and bubble-gum girl just stared at me.

"HE DIED?!" she asked, her voice rising in alarm, and I glanced around and caught several members now looking our way.

"Yes. It was pretty sudden. Did you know him?" I could now feel tears welling in my eyes and gritted my teeth to halt them.

"Oh my God, of course I did! He was a little hellion . . . always came in with that David kid. I'm so, so, so sorry!" Now she looked like she was about to cry, and I wasn't sure if I should reach out to her, get my card back, or just turn around and run. "Well, of course you can use his membership. Don't worry about anything at all, sweetie. Is there anything else I can do?"

"Thank you . . . no. Thanks so much for your help." I desperately just wanted to grab my card and get out of there at this point. She gave me a sympathetic look and I pushed my way through the entrance into the women's locker room, card clutched in my sweaty palm.

Spinning class took the place of yoga as my primary mode of exercise, and I came to crave that dark room where I could just go and block everything out. On the bike, no one knew my brother or me, so I could escape the "I'm-so-sorry-for-you" looks that I got so often from friends. I felt best in the dark, with beads of salty sweat dripping from my brow. At night I would nurse my sore muscles with hot showers and massage, cooking comforting meals that required just enough effort to take my mind off things for half an hour while I mixed, beat, and blended.

Despite it all, normal patterns began to return to our lives, slowly but surely. As my parents went back to their jobs and Rob began to finally feel comfortable leaving me at home by myself, I tried my hardest to just keep going. Writing heartfelt blog posts and responding to emails became a new routine that helped keep me grounded, and I was blown away by the outpouring of love and support by my readers. Care packages from foreign countries began to come to the door, as did book-length emails from girls telling me how much they admired my strength throughout the ordeal.

Numerous people—readers, and friends—asked if I would consider taking some sort of antidepressant to ease the trauma of the previous month, but I always refused. In college, I had gone through a brief period of depression (or what was diagnosed as depression) and had resorted to one of these medications for a year. Instead of helping me cope, it had merely numbed my brain and left me feeling strange and plasticlike. Now I wanted to feel things, to really feel them for all they were, even if there was some pain, so instead of pills I just focused on staying busy. I threw myself into freelance writing, planning for a bloggers' conference, spinning, and cooking.

On the outside, I maintained the sunny disposition that I'm widely known for online; I kept on a big smile and laughed at all the right moments. On the inside, though, it felt like pieces were breaking off my heart, one crumb at a time. I've never been one to really express my feelings; whenever anyone asked me how I was doing, I just answered that I was fine, fine. Throughout my life I've always taken on a protector mode in times of trouble, and I told myself I had to keep it together for my family.

In May, one month after John's death, at the urging of my friend Christie, I took a spontaneous weekend trip to the South Carolina Lowcountry. I needed to get far away from Tampa. When, after six hours of driving nonstop, I finally entered the Charleston county lines, the sense of relief was so great that I started to cry. I rolled down the windows and took deep inhales of the salt and marsh and sea, and for the first time in a long time, I felt lighter.

When I was very young, we lived on the South Carolina coast for a short time. My brother was born on Hilton Head Island in the early nineties, and there was just something about the Lowcountry that had gotten into my soul and had never left. No matter what stage of life I'm in, that drive on Highway 17 from Beaufort to Charleston always feels like coming home.

As I drove on through West Ashley and approached downtown, I could see the Cooper River Bridge in the distance and the stately antebellum buildings of College of Charleston rise up in the sky. The scents of the ocean were replaced with aromas of roast oysters, shrimp, and incense. When I pulled my old black Honda into Christie's driveway on Vanderhorst Street, across the street from the college library where I had spent so many hours memorizing Shakespeare and studying Victorian literature, she came running out and gave me a long, comforting hug.

That weekend we soaked up Charleston culture, beaching ourselves on the warm sands of Folly, eating benne wafers at the French Market, and drinking far too much red wine at my favorite wine bar next door to my old apartment on King Street. We went shopping, ate frozen yogurt, and traded hysterical stories about high school and our tiny hometown that seemed a million miles away. At one point, I thought to myself, *Is it okay to laugh?* Laughing felt foreign and forced; it was as if deep, permanent lines of sadness had been etched into my once bright disposition. And when I stared at myself in the mirror in Christie's bathroom, I had no idea who the girl looking back at me was. I felt as if I had aged ten years in the past four weeks.

I mentioned this to Christie, and that night we both plastered our faces with mineral clay. Sitting on the bed with my best friend, I felt the strange, light feeling come over me again and started to giggle. Cracks appeared in the mud around my mouth, and all at once, I knew it was going to be all right. Maybe not right now or in the next few days, but someday things would be okay again. I could still laugh. Under the layers of grief and sorrow, I could find glimpses of the life I once lived. We washed off our masks with warm water, got dressed in sundresses and sandals, and headed out for dinner and drinks at a hole-in-the-wall French restaurant on Broad Street, the type of place that the snowbirds would never find, where only locals could appreciate the $4.50 glasses of house red wine.

"You know, you seem to be doing all right," Christie said as we clinked glasses and shared our favorite appetizer of escargot, the garlicky, buttery snails oozing on our forks.

"Some days I am . . . some moments I forget he's gone. It's like I'll totally forget what happened and order a pizza, half pepperoni, half cheese, the way he would like it, and then I remember and it's as if someone has punched me in the stomach." I stared at the couple sitting across from us, holding hands and talking in hushed Southern voices.

"Sometimes I still feel guilty; I wish I could have been a better sister; I wish we hadn't fought so much." Memories of the final day began to surface: my yelling at John to get a life and John slamming the door behind . . . for the last time. I was supposed to help him write his college admissions essay; the document was still sitting unedited on my laptop, breaking mid-sentence. I caught my breath and pushed a strand of hair behind my ear, tucking it neatly and out of sight. Christie took a sip of wine and looked at me.

"Jenna, you were a great sister. Brothers and sisters fight all the time, you know that. John knew how much you loved him."

I looked down at my wrist. Two weeks after his death, I'd gone with my family to get tattoos, a very atypical bonding experience for us all. John had wanted to get a tattoo for his nineteenth birthday, a cross on his back saying "give me strength" across it. His death was only a week and a half after his birthday, and he'd never gotten around to getting inked. So we found it fitting to do it in his place. Until the tattoo, I was relatively numb, but as that needle dug in over and over into the soft flesh of my wrist, I felt a sense of satisfaction in the pain. I rubbed the blue cross now as Christie spoke, as if to wear it in farther.

Our food came then, plates of delicious fish fresh from coastal waters and vegetables dotted with butter and sea salt. We each ordered more wine, and our conversation became quicker and more lighthearted as we shifted topics, starting to discuss what our high school classmates were doing with their lives six years later. Christie told me how our friend Mary was already pregnant with her third child, and my high school boyfriend was thinking about getting engaged to a girl he had met in college.

Other than eating, we spent our time over the next few days taking incredibly long walks all around the city and down near the water, admiring the magnificent hundred-year-old Charleston homes. I loved the feel of my sandals on the cobblestones and the sunshine on my face.

Christie, recently having graduated from law school, was in the midst of studying for the bar exam, so one day while she studied, I made my way to my old yoga studio to see if a class might finally bring me some peace. The studio was so comfortably familiar, and as I looked in the mirrors that lined the walls, I could see for the first time how my grief was affecting my physical self. Over the past five weeks, I had lost about ten pounds. I had always been slender and the loss was not flattering on my frame; my collarbone and backbone protruded sharply. There's no real way to explain my weight loss other than grief. I had eaten my fair share of cookies and cakes brought over by the church and neighbors, finding solace in the sweet crumbs and icing. Despite all I ate, though, I continued to lose weight. It was as if my sadness and grief took the place of the gym in burning calories. I took this as a sign to eat all the delicious Southern food I wanted on my little vacation, and eat I did.

My absolute favorite Charlestonian dish is shrimp and grits. A standard on the menu of pretty much every Charleston restaurant, this comforting one-pot meal is said to have nourished shrimpers and sailors as a hearty early-morning breakfast before they headed out to sea. I like mine for dinner, with plenty of hot sauce on the side.

Lowcountry Shrimp and Grits

Serves 4

Although this dish was traditionally served for breakast to shrimpers coming into shore after long weeks out at sea, it's one of my favorite comfort foods for dinners. Look for applewood-smoked bacon, or ask your butcher to cut your bacon extra thick.

¾ cup stone-ground grits (dry)
12 slices bacon (preferably applewood smoked)
2 tablespoons diced leeks
½ onion, chopped
1 green pepper, diced
1½ pounds medium to large shrimp, peeled and deveined
¼ cup white wine
2 cups half-and-half
Salt and pepper to taste
Chopped green onion for garnish
Hot sauce

Cook the grits according to package directions. Remove from heat but keep covered on the stove while you prepare other ingredients.

In a cast-iron skillet over medium heat, fry the bacon. When bacon is crispy, remove from skillet and crumble onto a small plate. Add leeks, onion, and green pepper to the hot bacon grease and cook over medium high heat until soft and translucent. Add shrimp and sauté for about a minute or so, until they turn pink (be careful not to overcook!).

Remove shrimp from skillet. Add white wine to deglaze, then stir in half-and-half and bring mixture to a simmer. Continue to simmer sauce until it starts to thicken, about 2 minutes. Add shrimp to sauce and season with salt and pepper.

Divide cooked grits among four bowls. Ladle shrimp and sauce over grits. Sprinkle with chopped green onions to garnish and serve with plenty of hot sauce.

Benne Seed Sugar Cookies

Makes about 2 dozen cookies

A Charleston classic, these sesame seed cookies are both simple and elegant. They are perfect for an afternoon snack with a cup of herbal tea.

½ cup sesame seeds
1 stick (8 tablespoons) butter, softened
1 cup packed dark brown sugar
2 eggs
1½ cups flour
¼ teaspoons baking powder

Preheat the oven to 350° F. Line two baking sheets with parchment paper.

Toast sesame seeds on a baking sheet for about 5 minutes, shaking occasionally, until golden.

In a bowl, cream together butter and brown sugar. Add eggs, one at a time, and then add flour and baking powder. Fold in sesame seeds.

Using an ice cream scoop or spoon, scoop out large balls of dough onto lined baking sheets.

Bake for 15 minutes, or until bottoms of cookies are golden.

20

UNEXPECTED TRAVELS

I WAS NOT READY TO LEAVE CHARLESTON. GOING HOME AND once again facing my brother's empty room was almost too great a burden to bear. On my short trip, I found that I really didn't miss anything at home. I was ready to get away for good, to spread my wings and start over. But of course I couldn't hide out in Charleston forever, and so I cried as I crossed the bridge leading back over to West Ashley and away from the marsh and salt air that my body craved. I made my way back down through the Lowcountry, through Georgia and the Florida panhandle, watching through oversized sunglasses as the black asphalt spun beneath the car, bringing me closer to home. I debated listening to the audio book that I had purchased for the returning leg of my journey but decided instead to drive mostly in silence with my own thoughts. I already missed Charleston and kept feeling the urge to pull a U-turn in the middle of the highway and head back north.

I finally made it to Tampa later that evening and headed to Rob's apartment, where I had been staying since the accident.

"How was it?" he asked over a glass of wine as I unpacked my suitcase, sand from the beach falling out of it and onto the wood floor.

"Great," I responded. "So good to get away and be with Christie again . . . it felt like going home." I winced after I said this, because with him, in Tampa, was supposed to be my home. The home I had been planning on coming back to for years, while I was away in college, in France, and at culinary school. How is it that nothing ever feels the way you expect it to feel? Sometimes, the anticipation of a place is better than the reality. When I looked up, I realized Rob was staring at me and once again, I had been lost in my own deep thoughts.

"Sorry I'm not more talkative, I'm just exhausted right now. Christie and I stayed up late last night, and then driving all day today . . . "

"You and Christie are quite the pair! I hope y'all didn't get in too much trouble together," Rob said with a smile.

I leaned over and kissed his cheek and told him I was going to go take a bath and write for a little while in bed. I closed the bathroom door gently and immediately started to cry on the other side, pressing a cool washcloth to my face in an effort to hide the splotches that soon appeared on my cheeks. Soon, however, the tears became more of a silent heaving sob and I ran water in the tub, sat down in it, and drew my knees up close to my chest as I cried. Thoughts of my brother's death led to more dark thoughts; I just missed him so much.

"Jenna? Are you okay?" Rob's voice appeared on the other side of the door, and I realized I had been sitting in the bathtub for an hour. The water was now cool, my fingers wrinkled and pruned. I stood up and let the water fall off me, making little puddles on the floor.

"Yep, I'm fine! I must have fallen asleep in the bath. Hang on a sec." I wrapped a towel tightly around me, wiped my face, and opened the door.

"I thought I heard you crying. Were you crying in there?" he asked, his face showing concern.

"Oh, no. I'm fine. I'm really just exhausted right now, so I think I'm going to head to bed. Good night." I got in bed, fell asleep quickly, and, for the first time in a long time, did not dream.

The next day Rob emailed me from work, telling me about an amazing job listing he'd seen. At the moment I got the email, I was sitting in the condo and wondering how in the world I was going to make a living. The days were getting longer and I spent them cooking at home, answering blog emails, and sitting in front of my laptop, on Monster.com, just waiting for something to happen.

The dream job was for a position blogging about wine out in Sonoma County—it might as well have been a different country. I'd never been to California before, and the distance and foreignness of the state allured me more than anything else. I knew I needed a change, something totally different. I was flailing in Tampa; everything about home reminded me of my brother. I would have dreams that he was drowning in the pool and I couldn't save him. I tortured myself with memories and ate way too much banana bread in the process. The sound of sirens set off panic attacks in the middle of the night.

So, when Rob's email came in that Tuesday morning in May, I stared at the computer screen for a few minutes and then headed over to my parents' house to have my mom record my video application. Later I would look back and cringe that I hadn't spent more time thinking about my application before making it, but when I set my mind to something there's no stopping me.

We recorded the video, with me reading cue cards and dressed up in a chef's uniform (don't ask me what I was thinking), and then ate enormous Greek salads as I called my dad and told him about the position. I stabbed iceberg lettuce and wedges of salty feta on my fork as I explained the details to my dad. And then I basically forgot about the whole thing, writing it off as a one-in-a-million chance that anything would ever actually happen.

You can imagine my surprise when, only a few weeks later, I got an email from the winery, telling me I had a preliminary phone interview. I was so nervous on the phone that I said some things I shouldn't have—I think I even blurted out that in general I really don't like California Chardonnay—but for some reason it didn't throw me out of the running. In fact, to my even further surprise, I went on to make the cut for the top fifty and, later, the final top ten.

When I found out, I was standing in my kitchen and screamed out loud. The first call I made was to my dad; neither of us could believe it. In only a week and a half I would be jetting off to wine country for a weekend-long final interview (which would basically double as a paid vacation). Regardless of whether or not I got the dream job, I knew I was meant to go to California for this interview. Something in me was just one hundred percent certain that the trip was going to change my life. True, I was scared out of my mind, but I was also filled with the excitement of the unknown.

In the days preceding my trip, I practiced a lot of yoga and ate comforting foods to calm my nerves. Whenever I'm stressed, I automatically turn to yoga and baking—especially bread making. Kneading the dough, digging my hands into a raw life force, always gives me comfort and ease. I think that's why I took to baking in the first place.

And so, still brokenhearted and filled with loss and ache, I kissed Rob good-bye and boarded a plane for San Francisco.

Old-Fashioned Potato Rolls

Makes about 30 rolls

There's nothing quite as rewarding as making homemade bread, potato rolls especially! These are the fluffiest rolls I've ever tried. Serve them warm with honey and butter. They are best eaten the same day they are baked.

1 large russet potato
1 package (¼ ounce) dry yeast
¼ cup warm water (about 100°F)
2 eggs
⅔ cup sugar, divided
4½ cups flour, divided
1 teaspoon salt
1 stick (8 tablespoons) unsalted butter, at room temperature
1 egg plus 1 tablespoon warm water for egg wash

Bring a large pot of water to a boil on the stove. Peel potato, cut into uniform chunks, and cook for about 20 minutes until tender. Drain potato and transfer to a large bowl. Mash with a fork or potato masher.

Dissolve yeast in the warm water. Add eggs and ⅓ cup sugar to the mashed potatoes, then add the yeast/water mixture. Mix well to combine.

Add 2 cups of the flour and the salt to the potato mixture and mix with a wooden spoon until a wet, shaggy dough forms. Place a dishcloth over the bowl and set bowl in a warm spot (I use the top of the dryer) to rise for 1½ hours.

Beat the softened butter and the remaining ⅓ cup sugar in a stand mixer until smooth and creamy. Add risen dough and continue to beat with paddle attachment (or dough hook if you have one), adding the remaining 2½ cups flour slowly, until all flour has been incorporated and dough is pulling away from sides of mixer bowl. Keep mixing on high for 6 more minutes, until dough is no longer sticky to the touch (it will still stick to the sides of the bowl). Spray a large, clean bowl with cooking spray and place dough in it. Cover and let dough rise for another hour, until doubled in size.

Butter a 13- by 9-inch pan. Divide dough into about 30 small balls and place in dish. Cover and let rise (one last time!) for 45 minutes.

Preheat oven to 375°F.

Whisk egg and warm water. Brush rolls with egg wash and bake until golden, 35 minutes.

Simple Greek Salad

Serves 6

Maybe it's the salty olives or feta cheese, but every so often I just have to make this salad. It's also delicious with grilled chicken pieces, chopped rotisserie chicken, or grilled shrimp on top!

½ red onion, sliced
½ cup pitted kalamata olives
1 can artichoke hearts
1 large cucumber, peeled and chopped
6 ounces cubed feta cheese
4 large basil leaves, torn
2 tablespoons extra-virgin olive oil
2 tablespoons red wine vinegar
1 teaspoon dried oregano
½ teaspoon sea salt
½ teaspoon freshly ground black pepper

In a large bowl, toss together all ingredients. Transfer to the refrigerator and let marinate for at least an hour before serving.

21

NEW FRIENDS

STANDING ALONE IN THE AIRPORT, AFTER THE FIRST CROSS-country flight of my life, I heard my name echo over the baggage-claim intercom. "Jenna Weber," a nasal voice said, pronouncing my name *Wee-ber* instead of *Weh-ber*, "please meet your party at carousel number seven." I whirled around and came face to face with a college-age, blond-haired, blue-eyed boy wearing jeans and a red polo shirt. He was completely loaded down with fancy camera equipment and looked like he had just stepped out of either a fraternity house or an Abercrombie & Fitch photo shoot.

"Hey, I'm Rocky Slaughter," he said with a grin and extended his hand.

"I'm Jenna," I responded. "Is Rocky a nickname?"

Rocky laughed. "Nope! It's one hundred percent legit. I'm going to be the president someday."

"Oh really? Well, I'll watch out for you then. Wow, that's a ton of gear you have there!" I said, pointing at his stuffed camera bag and suitcase.

"Yeah, well, I wasn't sure what exactly to bring so I just brought it all! I'm most excited about this, though," Rocky said, holding up a briefcase with the words "Murphy-Goode Box of Tricks" written on the front. "I had all these ideas back in Boston, and I thought even if I'm not the person chosen for the job, these things would benefit someone!"

His enthusiasm was contagious, and I felt suddenly overcome with giddiness. I was out of my shell, out of that condo, and out of Tampa. California was someplace entirely new and seemed to be a place where anything could be made possible.

Murphy-Goode had a car and driver waiting for us, and Rocky and I chatted the whole way up to wine country. I stared out the window in awe as we crossed over the Golden Gate Bridge and over the rolling hills that separated the bay from the ocean. When we finally arrived at our destination, in the town of Healdsburg, we checked into the posh Hotel Healdsburg on the square and took in our surroundings. Healdsburg was cute and quaint, with ivy-covered buildings, cafés that opened up into the street, and a big park with shady trees and benches. In the hotel lobby, I ran into a few of the other finalists, who were checking in as well.

I had done my homework on everyone before I came, and after staring at Facebook pictures for so long, I felt like I already knew them. We were all about the same age, except for James, who was my parents' age and seemed like the loner of the group. Most of all, I clicked almost immediately with Adam, a 26-year-old guy from Austin, Texas, with blond hair, hazel eyes, and an open, laid-back demeanor. He was the one I'd been most eager to meet because we'd appeared to have the most in common.

After briefly chatting with everyone, I headed up to my room to take a shower and freshen up for the big opening-night dinner. My luxurious hotel room featured a huge king-size bed, hardwood floors, a balcony, and a bathroom with quite possibly the largest hotel tub I had ever seen, complete with spa products and a bath pillow. There was a basket on the bed with my name on it containing a bottle of Chardonnay (ironically), a map of Healdsburg, and a letter from Greg, the winemaker at Murphy-Goode, welcoming us.

The initial giddiness I'd felt in the airport was quickly turning into exhaustion, and I could feel my eyelids beginning to droop. In my room, I threw open the door to my private balcony and took deep, grounding breaths of fresh air, filling my lungs with this place. For months I had sat stagnant, grief and depression weighing down on me, but now, as I drank in that sweet California breeze, I felt lighter.

Around 6:30 p.m. I walked across the street to the Murphy-Goode tasting room for dinner. I had butterflies in my stomach and desperately needed a glass of wine. The entire group was already there, sipping red wine and exchanging casual introductions. I gratefully accepted a glass of Merlot from the bartender and made my way into the circle.

I could already tell that Carrie and I would be good friends based on what I knew about her from some preliminary Facebook research. She was fun and outgoing, with beautiful Hawaiian features. We both were runners, and she reminded me of my group of friends from high school. Our conversation flowed easily. Julia, the only other woman in the group, was a bit harder to connect with. A trim blonde hailing from Los Angeles, she had a preternatural tan and a dominating personality, all theatrics and humor. Julia had previously had a TV show on Animal Planet. She was the type of woman I always envied— the kind who could work a crowd and make jokes, unafraid of making a fool of herself.

The other applicants—Rich, Casey, Mark, and David—were talk-ingamongst themselves in the corner of the tasting room. I had some preconceived notions about Casey based on his goofy application video, but I didn't really know what to think of Rich, Mark, or David. They all seemed nice but were the most reserved of the group so far, and I wondered what their stories were.

Out of everyone, I still found myself drawn to Adam the most. He had a gentle manner and a soft accent that reminded me of home, and the way he looked at me brought on a new feeling that I couldn't really describe. For the past three and a half years I had never looked twice at another guy and considered myself a fiercely loyal girlfriend. I couldn't quite identify it, but there was something about Adam that drew me in and made me feel like I had known him for years, and we had yet to even have a real conversation. Of course, we both had significant others at home and certainly weren't looking to start anything new, especially not here in these seemingly bizarre circumstances. More than anything, Adam just seemed like someone I wanted to get to know, and I was glad this interview had brought us to the same place at the same time.

While we ate, wine and conversation flowed freely. After every-one had chatted for a bit, one of the owners of the winery asked each of us to introduce ourselves with a two-minute speech. As I watched the other applicants step forward and speak of their many accomplish-ments, I realized what an extreme privilege it was to be among such a talented group of people. The application video that had gotten me this far was really nothing special compared to the highly advanced multi-media presentations used by my new friends, and I felt self-conscious.

I dreaded my speech and took a few long sips of red wine. Finally, when my name was called (last), I made my way to the front of the room, anxiously wiping my sweaty palms on my pale blue dress. I joked around a bit to start, and then, after my nerves calmed down a little bit, talked about the sorrow of the past couple months, my need to escape Florida, and how social media and my blog had helped me cope with the grief.

"I made the decision on the day that my little brother died to live each day to the absolute fullest and never take anything for granted again," I said in conclusion. "You only get one chance at life, and I want to live without regrets, doing what I love. Life is way too short to do something you aren't passionate about."

Even though we all had just met only a few hours before, I felt like I truly connected with this group of people. It seemed like life had brought us together for a bigger purpose than a job interview. The atmosphere in the room relaxed after all the introductions were out of the way, and Greg, the winemaker, stepped forward to read out the "teams" for the weekend.

If I ever had any preconceived idea of what winemakers were like, Greg totally blew them all out of the water. He was young, probably in his mid-thirties, with facial hair and the solid build of a football player. He was wearing a T-shirt, faded jeans, and cowboy boots. Everything that came out of his mouth was hysterical, and I found myself not terribly surprised when he casually threw in that he used to follow the Grateful Dead.

I was placed on a team with Adam. We immediately started plotting what we would serve the group, since we both loved to cook.

The rest of the team—Julia, David, and James—seemed less than enthusiastic.

After the last bit of wine was drained from the bottles, Greg said, "I don't know what you guys are doing, but I'm headed next door to the bar. It would probably be a good idea for everyone to follow!" My body still felt shocked from the time change, and my head was feeling a little fuzzy from all the wine, but I knew I couldn't be the only one to call it a night.

"You look tired," Adam said as we walked across the street to the Healdsburg Bar and Grill for late-night bocce ball and pitchers of beer. The temperature outside had dropped alarmingly, and I wished I had thought to bring my sweater, but it had been well over ninety degrees when I walked across the street for dinner.

"Yeah, I'm exhausted. This is my first time to the West Coast, and I'm feeling the effects of jet lag right now."

"I'm beat, too, and I actually feel like I'm getting sick, so I don't really want to stay out that long," he said. "How 'bout we just stay for two games and then walk back to the hotel?" I was grateful for someone to walk back with so I didn't have to feel lame going home early by myself.

"Sounds good. I could use a good night's sleep tonight. I woke up this morning at 3:30 a.m. California time to catch my plane." I looked at my watch and realized that that was almost 24 hours ago. Exhaustion hit me like a ton of bricks.

For the next hour, I mustered enough energy to keep up with the group. Two rounds of bocce ball later, Adam and I looked at each other and he nodded.

"So, you're from Tampa," Adam said as we walked back across the street.

"Well, not originally. I grew up in a really small town on the east coast of Florida . . . but I'm sure you never have heard of it. Vero Beach?"

Adam shook his head. "I'm sure you've never heard of my hometown either. It's a very small town in East Texas that has a population of only about five hundred. I bet that beats Vero!"

I laughed and wondered how it was that already I felt so comfortable with this almost-total stranger. Conversation came easily, and nothing felt awkward or forced. "You're right . . . you win. Vero is pretty small, though. I like to refer to it fondly as a retirement community. We get a ton of snowbirds there." By this time we had reached the hotel and were at the door to my room.

"Well, good night. I guess I'll see you in the morning then," Adam said as I turned to open the door to my room.

"Good night! Hope you feel better!" I responded and closed the door behind me, taking it all in. I came to California with no prior expectations because this whole experience was just so out of the ordinary, but now I couldn't help but think about what was going to happen the rest of the weekend, and my thoughts raced.

I didn't sleep at all. The bed was the most comfortable I had ever been on, and the sheets were smooth as spun silk, but all night long I tossed and turned. Finally, around six o'clock, I got up and stumbled in an exhausted daze to the shower. I was due at the tasting room in an hour, and from there we were going to head up to Alexander Mountain as a group to learn more about the grapes and the vineyard. After that, we would have lunch and an afternoon activity, followed by dinner and games. Tonight wasn't my group's turn to make dinner, and I looked forward to just relaxing and getting to know everyone better.

Downstairs I ran into James sitting by himself with a cup of coffee.

"Do you mind if I sit?" I asked as I gestured to the empty chair across from him.

"Nope, feel free." he said, putting his paper down. "Last night was crazy, huh? I think I'm a little too old for this group!" James was turning fifty but appeared to be ten years younger, with a pierced ear and facial hair. We made small talk for the next five minutes or so before he stood up and excused himself. It was almost as if he was uncomfortable sitting with me, and I felt a little unsettled after he left, wondering if I had said something wrong.

The breakfast buffet at the hotel was set up with a huge spread, and I filled my bowl with creamy plain yogurt and topped it with golden granola and a few pieces of juicy pineapple. The granola was amazingly rich, almost as though the individual flakes of oat had been pan-fried in coconut oil. It had an abundance of cinnamon and honey, and big pieces of crunchy almonds topped off the whole thing. I wondered briefly if I could purchase this granola at the front desk; I had never tasted anything quite as good in Florida.

I never was able to find that granola, but with a little effort in the kitchen back home, I created my own version that is *almost* as good.

Golden Granola

Makes about 8 cups

I like to use lots of nuts in this, but feel free to substitute whatever you like for your own variation. This granola will keep for about three weeks in a sealed plastic container in the fridge, making it a quick and easy breakfast when topped with thick yogurt and banana slices.

1 cup maple syrup or honey
3 tablespoons coconut oil
1 teaspoon vanilla extract
2 cups old-fashioned oats
½ cup chopped hazelnuts
½ cup unsalted sunflower seeds
½ cup slivered almonds
2 teaspoons cinnamon
Sprinkle of sea salt

Preheat the oven to 325°F and grease a large baking sheet.

In a small saucepan, combine the maple syrup (or honey) and coconut oil and bring to a simmer over low heat. Simmer for about 4 minutes, stirring constantly (do not splash). Remove the pan from the heat, stir in the vanilla extract, and set aside.

In a big bowl, stir together the oats, hazelnuts, sunflower seeds, almonds, cinnamon, and sea salt. Drizzle with the hot syrup and stir well to coat.

Spread granola mixture evenly on prepared baking sheet and bake, stirring frequently, until the granola has turned a golden color, about 20 minutes. Remove from the oven and let cool.

Store the granola in sealed plastic containers in the refrigerator for up to 3 weeks.

22
STRANGE ELECTRICITY

THE REST OF THE DAY WAS SPENT GOING NONSTOP. I ignored my exhaustion and started to run on pure adrenaline as we hiked to the top of Alexander Mountain, drank Merlot from paper cups, and stared at the valley below. The views were breathtaking and unlike anything I had ever seen before in the South. After a lunch of grilled eggplant sandwiches on chewy foccacia bread, I made my way back upstairs to my room to lie down for an hour before our late-afternoon activity began. We were assigned to pour wine in the tasting room for guests, presumably a task aimed at assessing our people skills.

Indeed, the tasting room was filled with people when I arrived. I found one of the staff members and asked where I would be stationed. She ushered me to the back of the room and told me that Adam and I were to pour Merlot together for the next two hours.

"Hey!" Adam called out as I got myself situated behind the counter. "Looks like it's you and me again."

I laughed. "Yep, they must think we work well together or something. So what exactly are we supposed to be doing? Just pouring and mingling with people?"

"Yeah, we're going to meet a bunch of people," he said. "I hope you don't mind that I'm live-streaming this on the website I made for the trip—I thought it would be cool to show us actually 'working.'" Then his tone grew more serious. "I know this isn't the best time to talk about this, but I also wanted to tell you how sorry I am about your brother. I read about him online. What a terrible tragedy." He looked down at the tattoo on my wrist. "I love your tattoo."

"Thanks," I said. "It's been really hard, but I just try to stay busy . . . " I let myself trail off. "It's hard to explain."

"Tell me about it. My girlfriend passed away a few years ago. I know it's not the same as a sibling, but I sort of know how you feel. It sucks." Adam's voice was sincere and he looked me straight in the eyes.

"Gosh, I'm sorry. I had no idea. I can imagine. But you're right; I guess you do sort of know how I feel. It's hard to explain to someone who's never lost anyone close to them." I looked away because I felt like at any moment I might start to cry.

"Anyway, I just wanted to tell you that. We should chat further this weekend. I feel like we have a lot in common."

"I'd like that. Shouldn't be so hard, since these folks have paired us together for basically everything!" I said, laughing, before turning to a customer who had just set his empty wineglass on the counter before me.

The next two hours flew by as Adam and I worked together, chatting with customers and telling many of them about our interview process. By the time five o'clock rolled around, I was tired of being on my feet and was thankful for the hour to rest before cocktails and dinner. I secretly hoped I would run into Adam again in the lobby before heading to dinner, but he was nowhere to be found. I couldn't even remember the last time I felt so connected with someone, and I ached for more conversation.

Dinner was created by Team One and consisted of juicy mini-hamburgers stuffed with creamy goat cheese, grilled vegetables, chicken schnitzel, and an Asian-style cucumber salad, prepared by Rocky, who, it turned out, had a major flair for Japanese cuisine. Our glasses were filled to the brim with Murphy-Goode's signature Zinfandel, Liar's Dice, and we sat outside the house that the future employee would live in.

I thought of Rob back home. He continued to be incredibly sweet and encouraging, and I felt a tiny stab of guilt for feeling attracted to Adam. I didn't even *know* Adam, but I wondered if perhaps he felt the strange bit of electricity when talking to me, too. The night was capped off with a round of liar's dice, the game the wine was named after. Around midnight I said good night to all my new friends and headed back to my hotel room, where I slept for the first time in California.

Sunday was the final day of the weekend activities and also the day of our big interviews. Somehow I was picked to go first, and I was glad to get it out of the way. I had bought a new dress for the occasion and was downstairs eating my new favorite granola with yogurt and a hard-boiled egg when Adam walked by.

"I've been up since 5:30 this morning filming this clip with Greg and Casey," he said. "I just wanted to say good luck! I'll be interested to hear how it goes. I'm going last."

"Thanks! I'm actually pretty glad that I'm going first and then have the whole day to relax," I replied. "The hotel pool might be calling my name."

Adam laughed. "Well, I'll catch you later. Here's my number if you want to grab something to eat when you're done." He wrote on a napkin, and I punched the number into my Blackberry.

The interview was pretty standard. I got asked a bunch of questions about the blog and how I felt I could best promote the company if I were given the job. Interviews have always been one of my strengths, and I ended this one as I always do, with a firm handshake like the one my dad taught me when I was a little girl.

I thought about calling Adam afterward to tell him how it went, but I held off and called Rob instead. He answered after one ring with an excited tone. "Hey! How did it go? I bet you rocked it. I miss you so much!"

"Hi!" I responded. "It went well, I think. I'm just glad I went first. I got to say everything I wanted to say and feel pretty good about it."

"That's fantastic. They would be crazy not to want to hire you."

"Well, don't get your hopes up. Regardless, this has been such a great experience and I feel like I've made some really good friends!" I almost mentioned Adam but bit my tongue. Technically there was nothing between us, and of course I was *allowed* to have friends who were guys, but I decided not to even go there. "Hey, Babe, I gotta run though. I'm starving and then have to meet with my group about cooking tonight."

"Okay, I love you!" Rob said, and I clicked my phone shut.

I decided to grab a sandwich on my own and headed over to Oakville Grocery, a homey spot with a large outdoor fireplace and a wine bar inside. All the sandwiches looked delicious, and I was suddenly famished. I chose chicken and Gruyère on a French baguette, and while I was sitting outside my phone buzzed with a text message from Adam. *Just finished my interview. Starving . . . lunch?* I replied to tell him where I was and then sat back in my chair in the sunshine.

"Hey!" he called as he walked up to the table. "I'm so hungry . . . let me go inside and grab a sandwich." He came back about ten minutes later with the same sandwich I had ordered and a bottle of iced tea. Noticing me squinting in the sun, he handed me his red aviator sunglasses. I put them on and smiled.

"So, how did it go?" I asked as he dug into his sandwich.

"Great! My approach is to just always be myself in situations like that. This is just between us, but I think there might be a few other opportunities open for us other than this Murphy-Goode job," he said.

"You think? Like what?" I asked him.

"Well, I don't know exactly . . . but they sort of hinted to me that there was something else available. Let's just say tomorrow will be very interesting. By the way, this sandwich is amazing. Do you want a bite?"

"No thanks; I actually just finished the same thing. I love Gruyère!"

We sat outside for another twenty minutes discussing the dinner we were going to make for the group that evening. It turned out we would be cooking for twenty-five people, which was more than I ever had cooked for in the past. I suggested something that could easily be made for a large group, like risotto, and it went from there. Eric was also on our team and said he would make teriyaki steak; I would make my mushroom risotto, and Adam was in charge of dessert. I thought to myself that this was going to be really good. Having a degree in baking and pastry always made me very curious to taste other people's desserts, and as much as I hated to admit it, I usually judged them on it. Adam seemed to be good at whatever he did, so I was very curious to see how he managed on the dessert front.

Later that afternoon, Adam and I cooked alone in the kitchen while the rest of our group mingled outside. We both were quiet, focusing on our tasks at hand, but the silence wasn't awkward in the least. An hour or so later, we served the finished products to our guests, who raved about both the risotto and the Mexican cheesecake Adam had whipped up. *Hmmm,* I thought, *the guy can bake*! I made a mental note to later ask him to email me the recipe so I could re-create it at home.

The next morning was filled with nervous energy as the ten of us crowded under the tiny gazebo in the park, waiting for Dave to announce who had been chosen for the job. I laughed and joked with Rocky and Carrie and then we all took our seats and Dave picked up the mic.

"I can't even express what an awesome time it's been getting to know these ten talented people from around the country. I wish we could hire all of you, but my boss told me only one or else I lose my job." The crowd broke out in laughter. "So, without anything further, I'd like to welcome Casey as our new Wine Lifestyle Correspondent!"

We all broke out in applause as Casey stood up to give Greg a big hug. Honestly, I was only a little bit disappointed that I wasn't the one hired. Overall, I felt intense gratitude that I had made it this far and been able to take part in such a fun weekend. I gave Casey a hug afterward and knew that the absolutely perfect person had been chosen for the position. Then, suddenly, I felt an arm on my shoulder and looked up to see the face of one of the women on the PR team for Kendall-Jackson, another California winery owned by the same parent company as Murphy-Goode.

"Jenna, can I talk to you for just a moment?" she asked. I couldn't believe what she told me next. They wanted me to fly down to Southern California the next day to visit another Jackson family winery. My travel arrangements would be taken care of, and Adam would be accompanying me.

I waited about an hour before calling Adam to see what in the world was going on. Everyone else was going home that afternoon but we would be staying and traveling together the next day. It didn't even make sense. Adam answered the phone with excitement.

"Ready for tomorrow?" he asked.

"I have no idea what's going on!" I responded.

We chatted for a few minutes, and then I told him I was exhausted and going to bed early.

I said good-bye to all my new friends as they headed out and then ate a quiet dinner by myself at the little Vietnamese restaurant next door to the hotel. The noodle bowl was absolutely perfect and had big chunks of crispy spring roll mixed throughout, as well as peanuts, scallions, and wedges of lime. It might sound odd, but I've actually always enjoyed eating dinner by myself. I relish the entire process and usually bring a book to read while I wait for my food. I figure I either look like I have no friends or like a VIP restaurant critic, since I always take photos of my meals before eating. Either way, it works just fine, and after having such an intense and draining weekend, silence was my best friend.

Early the next morning, we left the hotel and drove to the small Sonoma County airport. I couldn't believe that I was actually flying down the California coastline in a private plane. It belonged to the owner of the company, Jess Jackson, and was fully stocked with blankets, granola bars, and big bottles of water for us. While Adam chatted with the Jackson family employees up front, I pressed my face against the window in the back and just took it all in. Never before had I seen natural splendor like the stretching miles of mountains and ocean that sprawled before me. Florida seemed like light-years away, and I felt something change from deep inside. I dreaded going back home to the cramped condo I now shared with Rob, dreaded returning to my old life, where it felt like I did the same old thing every day. Not that my life was ever bad, but after experiencing something so new and wonderful, I knew nothing at home would be the same.

We spent the day at the beautiful Cambria wine estate, hiking through the vineyards and getting a whole tour of the winery. Finally, that evening, they put Adam and me into a limo headed for the Los Angeles airport; it was time to go home. We stretched out in the back and I arched my neck to see the city's skyline through the smog.

"I don't even know what to think right now; that was just crazy!" I said to Adam as I jokingly snapped his photo.

"I know. Who knows what the future holds! Ashley was talking to me a little bit about some interesting job opportunities today on the plane, so we'll see. I love Austin, but California is such an adventure!" he said.

"They didn't really talk to me about anything job related, and I'm still not quite sure why I'm involved in all this but, hey, I'm not complaining," I said. "For my first time on the West Coast, I didn't do half bad!" I laughed, thinking how crazy it was that just one week earlier I had been so far removed from everything out here. I didn't even want to think about the red-eye flight I was about to take home.

The limo pulled up outside Adam's departure terminal, and I got outside to give him a hug good-bye.

"Well, who knows. Maybe I'll see you again one of these days in California!" he said. "Let's definitely keep in touch; I've got some good blogging ideas up my sleeve for you."

"Yeah, definitely. It was really great to meet you. Hopefully I'll see you again one day!" I said and then he grinned, threw his backpack on, and walked away. A few seconds later, he looked back over his shoulder at me, and I smiled good-bye before hustling inside.

I made my way into the busy airport and changed out of my nice jeans and blazer into more comfortable clothes for my overnight flight. I wondered if Adam had made his flight on time and thought to text message him, then realized I couldn't because he'd accidently left his cell phone out in the vineyards at Cambria.

The flight home was long and exhausting and made me realize just how far away I really had been. When we landed around six in the morning, Rob was there waiting for me with open arms. I fell into his embrace and wondered if perhaps the past four days had only been a dream. Tampa seemed hazy and humid, and I could still smell the hotel shampoo in my hair. When we finally got home and I fell into bed, I felt more tired than I ever had in my entire life. I slept all the way into the afternoon, and when I woke up I stumbled around the condo, feeling like something was missing, but I wasn't sure just what that was.

Mushroom Risotto

Serves 4

Making risotto is almost therapeutic for me, and during the chilly winter months I often enjoy making this for dinner. Served with a nice glass of red wine, it's all you really need. If you are not familiar with Arborio rice, it is a short-grained rice from Italy that has an especially high starch content. Nowadays, it is found in most supermarkets.

>   4 to 4½ cups homemade chicken stock (page 84)
>   1 tablespoon extra-virgin olive oil
>   1 shallot, minced
>   1 cup Arborio rice
>   ¼ cup dry white wine
>   1 tablespoon butter
>   16 ounces sliced cremini or baby bella mushrooms
>   ½ cup freshly grated Parmesan cheese

Heat the chicken stock in a small saucepan and keep warm over low heat. Heat the olive oil in a heavy-bottom pot over medium heat until hot but not smoking. Add the shallot and sauté for about 4 minutes, or until tender and translucent. Add the rice and stir well to coat. Cook for 3 minutes, stirring occasionally. Add the white wine and cook until all is absorbed, stirring constantly.

Continue to cook the rice, adding the chicken stock, ¼ cup at a time (a ladle does this job nicely), stirring continuously over medium heat until the stock has been completely absorbed by the rice. Do not add more stock until the previous amount has been completely absorbed by the rice. Once all the stock has been incorporated, continue to cook until the rice is just cooked through.

In a separate pan, melt the butter and sauté the mushrooms until tender, about 8 minutes. Add the cooked mushrooms and cheese to the risotto, stirring until combined, and serve.

Adam's Mexican Cheesecake

Serves 8–10

Admittedly, this is not a fancy recipe, but it is so creamy and delicious and easy, I just had to share it with you. Look for refrigerated crescent rolls near the butter in your supermarket.

- **2 cans crescent rolls, divided**
- **2 (8-ounce) packages cream cheese**
- **1½ cups sugar, divided**
- **1 teaspoon vanilla**
- **1 stick (8 tablespoons) butter or margarine**
- **1 tablespoon cinnamon, or to taste**

Preheat oven to 350°F. Spray a 13- by 9-inch baking pan with cooking spray.

Press one can crescent rolls into pan.

In a medium bowl, combine cream cheese, 1 cup sugar, and vanilla until creamy. Spread mixture over rolls. Cover the cream cheese topping with the remaining can of rolls, pressing pieces together.

In a small saucepan, melt the butter over low heat and stir in the remaining ½ cup sugar and cinnamon until mixture is smooth. Pour over top and bake for 30 minutes.

Serve warm or at room temperature.

23

DISLODGING

IN THE WEEKS THAT FOLLOWED, I TRIED TO SETTLE BACK INTO MY life with Rob, but I knew something in me had changed. I went through the motions, tried to stuff myself back into the box that was my life in Tampa, spending the days by myself blogging from home and hanging out with Rob and his friends at night. But it felt empty; that feeling that something was missing kept nagging at me. It suddenly felt as if I was living my life stuck in a fog. Rob was so excited to have me back, but thoughts of California and new opportunities consumed me. Adam and I had kept in pretty frequent touch through email, and I couldn't help the strange feeling of connectedness I felt with him. It was as if I had known him forever, even though we had only met two weeks before.

In the end, I knew I couldn't stay in Tampa; I couldn't stay in that comfortable condo with the pool and the big kitchen and the man who loved me. It was hard to believe that just one weekend in California could bring about such a monumental shift, but looking back on it now, it's clear that things had been moving in that direction for months. Ever since John's death, I had felt increasingly smothered. I never loved Tampa, never really wanted to be there, especially with all of the memories of my brother that the town now held. And it wasn't that I didn't love Rob anymore; it was more like every day since I came home from California I felt like I was losing myself more and more. And the relationship you have with yourself is the one that you really can't afford to lose.

About a week after I got home, I made a dinner of oven-fried chicken with a homemade honey mustard glaze and a side of pan-roasted broccoli. When we sat down to eat, though, I barely said a word as I carefully separated the meat from the bone.

"You're pretty quiet tonight," Rob observed. "Everything okay?"

"Yep, everything is fine." I answered quickly. We both knew everything was not fine.

Finally, after moving my broccoli around from one side of the plate to the other, I started to cry.

"Jenna! What's the matter? Are you thinking about your brother?" Rob moved closer to me and put his arm around my shoulders. I felt horrible.

"I just . . . I just . . . " I couldn't seem to get functional words out. "Rob, I just am having second thoughts. About us. I'm sorry . . . I don't know what else to say."

Rob just looked at me in disbelief. "What in the world are you talking about?" he almost shouted. I looked down at my chicken and brushed away a tear.

"I don't know. I don't know. I just don't feel right. It's not you; it's me. Something is wrong with me. You're perfect and what every girl dreams about!" I wanted to hold him but he had moved away from me and was now standing near the kitchen.

"Can we just think about this rationally?" Rob asked. "You know you don't really want to do this, Jenna. We've been through so much together!"

"You're right." I said. "I don't know what's come over me. I think I just need to go to bed." I felt horrible, but maybe he was right. Maybe I would feel differently in the morning and realize what a fool I was being.

But as I slid into bed that night, I knew in my heart that it was over. There was no going back now; my heart's decision was made.

I told him the next morning. After he left for work, I packed up my some of my cookbooks that I kept at his condo, stacking one after another into brown paper boxes, ignoring all the tabs on the pages or the faded ink cursive that read *Rob loves this dish! His first turkey burger!* When he left that morning, I stood at the door with tears in my eyes but with nothing more to say, and he just turned his back and walked away.

Everything with Rob had always been so *easy.* I had never seriously thought that it wouldn't work out, and we were as comfortable with each other as old married couples. Everything about him was familiar.

So after ending things with him, I deeply missed that sense of comfort. I felt lost, felt like I was drowning. The idea of California became a life raft, and I held on to it tightly. Not just the idea of California, but also the idea of Adam. He and I had been communicating more frequently lately, and as much as I hated to say it, or even think it, I knew deep down what had really happened. I had met someone new, and the possibilities of the unknown were too tempting to resist.

When I returned back to the doorstep of my parents' house, cookbooks tucked under arm and pillow in hand, my mom let me in and wrapped me in her arms. "Matters of the heart," she said, "are never, ever easy." And then my friend Anne came over with three bottles of wine and chocolates and we sat on the carpet and I cried myself into laughter while listening to cheesy songs. I had no plan of what I was going to do, had no job, was basically broke, and now had just unofficially moved back in with my parents, which is pretty much every college grad's worst nightmare.

The next day I was back at Rob's condo, hastily packing up dishes, when the five plates I was holding slipped right out of my hand. Sharp pieces of china surrounded me as I sank to my knees and sobbed my eyes out amidst the mess. Who knew if I was making the right decision? I was scared out of my mind. I had just given up the kind of relationship that most people would kill for. I had comfort and safety with Rob, and he treated me like a princess, bringing home cupcakes if he thought I was down, always letting me pick the movie, and leaving love notes for me to find. I'm sure we could have made it work, gotten married, and lived semi-happily ever after.

During the next few weeks, I began to pack up my life. I didn't really have a plan, and it felt almost freeing, the way you feel after collecting a basket of fresh produce from the farmer's market and have a total blank canvas in front of you on which to create your own masterpiece. I started to feel more and more confident that I had made the right decision. I needed to get out of Florida. I knew I wanted to live in Healdsburg, in the town that had originally sparked something so deep in me in July. It was a small town, full of families and foodies, and I loved that it was close to both the ocean and the mountains. More important, there was a certain sense of peace there that my soul ached for. I felt like I could breathe, in a way I'd never experienced in Tampa.

I spent the next few months thinking about making the move and putting out feelers for jobs. I signed up to attend a food blogging conference in San Francisco in the fall, so I knew that I'd be able to visit California soon, even if I wasn't quite ready to move there. Then, one September day, my phone rang with a part-time job offer working at a different winery in Dry Creek Valley, only about fifteen minutes from Healdsburg. This winery was small and organic, and had apparently heard about me when I had been in California with Kendall-Jackson. Without even pausing to think, I said yes. Later that night, I took a deep breath before cancelling my return flight from San Francisco. With a click of the mouse, I had completely changed my life. I stared at the computer screen with my new flight email confirmation for about ten minutes, until my mom called me down for dinner.

Adam had also been offered a job in the wine industry and had accepted as well. Over the weeks our friendship had blossomed via long phone conversations and lengthy emails, and we both couldn't wait to spend more time getting to know each other and exploring Northern California together. Ironically, Rocky would be Adam's new intern, so the three of us would all be together again. Since the guys were moving there before I was, they offered to let me crash on their futon until I found a place of my own. I gratefully accepted, laughing to myself at the craziness of the situation.

In five days I would be taking my second-ever cross-country flight from Florida, this time to move my entire life. Funny, the thoughts that run through your mind when you are packing up your old life for a new one—the things that you keep, the things that define you, and the things that hold you back. Out of all my hundreds of cookbooks, I only packed five. I figured I could send for the rest later and didn't have space for everything. Also included in my "California pile" were old photos, journals, and poems; my favorite dresses, skirts, and T-shirts that formed a timeline of the past six years from sorority parties through culinary school; my yoga mat. Having my whole world reduced to objects felt surreal. I bundled myself up in my faded college sweatpants and an old T-shirt and padded down the stairs to enjoy one of my last meals at my parents' house: my mom's "famous" chicken enchiladas. She had been making them practically forever, and they never failed to comfort me, no matter the situation. Before I knew it, the big morning had arrived. My flight was leaving at 7 a.m. out of Tampa, and I was lugging along two fifty-pound suitcases stuffed to the very brim, a journal, my beat-up point-and-shoot camera, and a book of quotes by Paulo Coelho that a friend had given me for my journey. My dad insisted on being the one to drive me to the airport early that morning.

"Jennifer, you know your mother and I are very, very proud of you," he said, and I could hear the pain thick in his voice at the idea of losing one child exactly five months after he'd permanently lost the other.

"Dad, I'll be fine. Really. You guys have no need to worry . . . " I told him with confidence in my voice, trying to mask the fact that I, too, was terrified.

"You were never meant to be fenced in and you have so many extraordinary gifts. I guess it's just your turn to fly," he said. "We both know we can't keep you here even though we may want to! And you know you can always talk to us about anything, and we will always be here for you."

"I know. Thanks, Dad. It's going to be fine, I promise. You are only a phone call away, and I'll see you again before we know it." I said this without really knowing when the next time would be. We pulled into the terminal, and my dad stopped by the curb.

He lifted my suitcases from the trunk, and I hoisted my backpack up over my shoulders. "Well, I guess this is it!" I said and gave him a long, tight hug.

"You be safe now, you hear? I love you." My dad had tears in his eyes, and I realized that this was only the second time I had ever seen him cry.

"I love you, too. I'll call you this afternoon," I said and watched him walk away and get back into the car while I was left standing there with my life stuffed into two bags and a backpack, waiting for a plane to take me west.

Once on the plane, I sat back in my seat and took a very deep breath. I couldn't believe this was really it; I was really moving away on my own, to return only on holidays. I was going to start a whole new life in a place I had only visited once for a short weekend. I had nowhere to live. Never before had my life been so spontaneous . . . and scary. I pulled out the Coelho book and read as my plane crossed the sky.

Whenever we need to make a very important decision, it is best to trust impulse and passion, because reason usually tries to remove us from our dream, saying that the time is not yet right. Reason is afraid of defeat, but intuition enjoys life and its challenges.

My decision to leave everything I had known and move to California was purely based on passion and intuition. I had a feeling deep down that California was where I was supposed to be, and so I simply went. I felt remarkably the same as I did on my very first morning of Basic Skills class, when the kitchen was still quiet and I had lined up my sharp knives at my station and tied on my apron tight. I had no idea what I was getting myself into, but I knew that it was going to be a really great adventure.

ACKNOWLEDGMENTS

IT HAS ALWAYS BEEN MY DREAM TO WRITE THIS BOOK. THE journey hasn't been the easiest, but after three years of late nights, part-time jobs, and dozens chocolate chip cookies, I finally have something I am so very proud of. I couldn't have done any of it without my family and friends, who constantly believed in me even when I didn't believe in myself; my editors, who helped me become a better writer every day; and most of all, without all of you who continue to read my website every single day without fail, lift my spirits when I'm down, and always give me a reason to smile. I cannot thank you enough for your constant support and encouragement throughout this journey. From the bottom of my heart, thank you.

INDEX